Celebrate your single life!

*Un*married *not* *Un*loved

A no-nonsense approach to creating a successful single experience

Kathleen Valchuk

Unmarried not Unloved

A no-nonsense approach to creating a successful single experience

Kathleen Valchuk

Lichfield Publishing Company
Chicago, Illinois

Copyright 1998 by Kathleen Valchuk.
All rights reserved

No part of this publication can be reproduced, stored in a retrieval system or transmitted in any form by any means electronic, mechanical, photocopying, recording or otherwise without the expressed written permission of Lichfield Publishing Company, Suite 406C, 1360 N. Sandburg Terrace, Chicago, Illinois, 60610.

First Edition
ISBN 0-9665717-0-3

Layout and design by Plan II Publications Ltd. Chicago, Illinois
Printed in the USA

Published and distributed to the trade by:
Lichfield Publishing Company
Suite 406C, 1360 N. Sandburg Terrace
Chicago, Illinois, 60610
312-664-9145 Fax 312-664-9155

Desiderata ©1972 by Max Ehrmann. All rights reserved.
Reprinted by permission Robert L. Bell, Melrose, Mass. 02176

Excerpts on pages 80-81 from *Personal Adjustment, Marriage and Family Living* by Landis, J., Landis, M. et al. © 1975 by Prentice Hall, Simon & Schuster Education Group.
Used by permission.

Library of Congress Catalog Card Number: 98-92123.

Kathy Valchuk

This book is dedicated to
Dan G. Guyer, M.D.,
the therapist who helped me
to become the person I am
and to
Dolores Blanks,
my sister, my mentor, my friend,
who has shared years of wisdom
and laughter with me.

TABLE OF CONTENTS

	Introduction	9
1	What Being Single is All About	11
2	Attitude is Everything	17
3	Decision Making	24
4	Hassle Free Living	31
5	The Fine Art of Socializing	46
6	Social Networking	56
7	Creating a Social Network	63
8	Marriage and Mating	76
9	The Dating Dilemma	83
10	Attractiveness	91
11	Unattractiveness	103
12	The Place Where You Live	112
13	Attracting Men	120
14	Dating	133
15	Dating Ethics and Etiquette	155
16	Sexuality	172
17	Handling Heartbreak	186
18	Therapy — Do You Need It?	197
	Last Words	201

INTRODUCTION

The why behind this book is simple — there is a need for it. This book is needed because it presents a positive view of the single lifestyle. It's purpose is to help the single woman deal more successfully with being a single person and to enjoy her life on a daily basis with or without a "Significant Other," "Consenting Adult" or whatever she chooses to call members of the opposite sex.

This book is about choices. It is not about coping. Coping indicates a less than satisfactory adjustment to living. It is muddling through. It is surviving, not enjoying. The successful single woman wants more for herself.

This book will not change your life, only you can do that. What it will do is offer suggestions that may help you to make your life more satisfying.

Chapter 1
WHAT BEING SINGLE IS ALL ABOUT

Why do we think everyone has to be married? Why are there so many books telling people, especially women, how to get married? Marriage is an option. So is being single. Is one better than the other? Probably not. Perhaps it would be more productive to think of married and single as different, not better or worse, just different. To do this, one must define exactly what the single state is and what it is not.

Single simply means not married. This definition carries with it no sense of desperation to be married, no value judgments about the desirability of singleness as a way of living and, most importantly, it allows singleness to be a state of choice, not chance.

Saying one is single can mean any of the following:

- I do not have a spouse.
- I am happily dating one or more persons.
- I haven't had a date in a long time and I have a happy, fulfilling life.
- I'm living with someone.
- I do not have a desire to be married
- I expect to marry when I choose to do so.
- I have a full social life and a satisfying job.
- I have raised a family and I am now enjoying the freedom to further develop myself.

Single can be defined in as many ways as there are single people. In the United States, that includes 44 percent of the adult population. We can't tell how many of these people are single by choice, but we do know that below the age of 34, there are more single males than single females in every age group.

Statistics can be interpreted in any number of ways. And depending on one's perspective, the interpretation can be bleak or promising. For years we have heard that the middle-aged single woman has a greater chance of being held hostage by terrorists than she does of finding a husband. What an awful way to look at singleness!

Yet, singles of all ages take this view seriously and increase their frustrations and worries in the area of relationships with self and others. They begin to ask questions of themselves and others that become more and more negative and self-defeating. Why doesn't anyone want me? When will I meet someone I can marry? What if I never get married? How come all the "good ones" are married?

Next comes the self-blame. "There must be something wrong with me." What's wrong is not with you, but with the view you have of the single state. As long as one views being single as abnormal, one cannot enjoy it as a state of being. There comes to be a shame and embarrassment associated with one's own existence. Energies are used either to disguise one's singleness or to engage in a desperate search to find a mate and end the single state.

Despite what you may have been hearing and feeling, single does not have to mean:

- lonely
- desperate to find a mate
- unhappy and dissatisfied on a daily basis
- unwanted
- unloved
- constantly searching
- waiting for Mr. Perfect to show up
- settling for a less than satisfying relationship to avoid aloneness

Attitude is everything. You do have a choice. And given the choice of the two descriptive lists included in this chapter, which one would you prefer to apply to yourself?

Choosing a more positive view of being single is just the beginning. Next you must define for yourself what being successful as a single person means. For each of us, success may mean something different. Defining it is a very individual process. No one can do it for you. However, I can describe what being a successful single person means for me and that may provide you with some insight into what it is you want to be all about.

I am a successful single person because I am happy most of the time. I do not dwell on the negative in my life and I have found a way to remove most of the hassles of daily living from my life. By defining priorities and organizing my finances, work load and social commitments, I have eliminated many of the major problems. I no longer allow minor irritations to interfere with the enjoyment of a day. I can find something positive in every situation and I look for the lessons to be learned from even the most difficult situations like car accidents, flooded basements, stock market losses, whatever.

I am a successful single person because I look forward to and find enjoyment in each and every day of my life. I am reminded of a comment by a psychologist on a radio broadcast which went something like this — if you can get out of bed at least four days out of seven without anxiety or dread about what the day will bring, you are not a depressed person. I manage to awaken cheerfully and get out of bed looking forward to seven out of seven days each week. Every day brings new experiences and challenges that provide me with fun and learning and that contribute to my growth as a human being and my understanding of others.

I am a very social being with a full social calendar. Since I am an extremely outgoing person, this one is very important to my view of myself as a successful single person. Staying active socially might not be quite so important to those who are less outgoing but all of us need others in our lives and we need to participate in a variety of activities to keep us growing and enjoying.

I enjoy my own company and cherish my moments of aloneness. I see myself as a well-rounded individual with a variety of interests and activities. Some of them include others; some do not. I love to read and think, to do crossword puzzles, to meditate, to watch television. I enjoy sitting on my balcony and watching the activity taking place on the sidewalks and streets below. Going for a solitary walk not only gives me exercise, it provides me with an opportunity to ponder the wonder of my own existence. I thoroughly enjoy an evening of music and candlelight while viewing the panorama of city life outside my windows.

I like myself. This is probably the most important prerequisite for being a successful single person. I do not need others to validate me. I need them to share life with me. I have spent many years becoming the person that I am and I am in love with her. If you don't like you, how can you expect others to like you?

I enjoy a wide variety of people. I can find something interesting about almost anyone. I do not include or exclude people from my life on the basis of income, dress, employment, attractiveness, where they live or any of the superficial characteristics. I include or exclude people from my life according to the quality of human interaction we experience with each other. This allows me to know and enjoy many people who enrich my life in special ways. Through them, I am always learning and growing.

I enjoy my job. I am a teacher. It's what I am meant to do. It feels good to me and I do it well. For many years I taught sex education and parenting to high school students. I saw my work as worthwhile and believed I was making a significant contribution to the world. I enjoyed the interaction I had with teenagers and got a great deal of pleasure and satisfaction from watching them grow and develop. I now work part-time teaching driver improvement to adults who drive fleet vehicles. I travel throughout the United States and meet a variety of people in a wide range of circumstances. One week, I may be working with sales people and the next week, I might work with truck drivers. I have fun with each group. Since each of us who works will spend close to half of our waking hours on the job, shouldn't work bring some enjoyment to our lives? How can we be successful if we hate what we do most of every day?

Yes, I also enjoy days off and vacation periods. And I don't always want to go to work, but for the most part, I feel I get as much as I give to my job and that balance is important to my sense of happiness and well-being.

I am actively involved in my own life. I do not sit home waiting for the phone to ring. I create activities in my life that bring me enjoyment. I find the dynamics of human relationships fascinating and spend a lot of time learning through what goes on with myself and others in relationships. I am not a passive participant who waits for others to entertain me. Enjoying my life is my responsibility, not someone else's.

Finally, **I am not desperate to find a mate.** If I marry again, that would be wonderful. If I don't, my life will still be wonderful. My happiness and success as a person is not determined by whether or not there is a man in my life. I do enjoy dating and intimacy but can allow a relationship with a member of the opposite sex to unfold and become what it is going to be. I have even gone as long as two years without dating and have used the time to learn more about myself and the way I function in the world.

I have good friends of both sexes so I have male companionship whenever I want it. I still attend all of the social events I choose to bring fun into my life. Sometimes I go with a group, sometimes with a male or female friend and sometimes I choose to go alone.

As you read through the description of living that defines me as a successful single person, I hope you have been prompted to review and evaluate your own approach to life. If the approach I am suggesting sounds too simple, that's because it is. Who said that life has to be hard? Once you determine your own formula for successful living, everything else will fall into place.

Chapter 2
ATTITUDE
IS EVERYTHING

Ask any woman who is single and enjoys life how she feels about getting married. Those women who have found satisfaction in singleness will answer that while they have not ruled marriage out, it is no longer a primary goal in everything they do. If someone enters their life with whom they are able to find happiness and enjoyment, marriage is an alternative to be considered.

And therein lies the significant factor, the one that determines whether or not one can be happy as a single person. The satisfied single sees both marriage and singleness as choices. Marriage has not been ruled out, but it is not the focal point of every moment nor is it the purpose for all male-female relationships. It is rather only what it is — one of the options of one's life.

This book is about choices. If you are approaching it with the thought that you might as well learn how to be single because *no one acceptable to you* seems to want you (this idea will be explored later), you definitely need an attitude adjustment. If you see enjoying single life as a secondary or lesser choice to being married, your attitude will prevent you from living fully and finding the satisfaction that each and every day of your life can provide for you. If you look at being single as something you have to go through on your way to getting married, many of the opportunities for fully living your own life will be lost to you.

The real wonder of being single is that you get to decide the kind of single person you want to be. Happy, satisfied, socially active, attractive, friendly, enjoying each day or sullen, depressed, whining, complaining, negative, hopeless, angry, out-of-control.

Perhaps you have heard the statement that "she made herself up." Well, don't we all? Usually, when we use this statement, we are referring to someone who seems happy, successful and on top of the world. We think it's an act. It's not, and even if it is, so what? If you play a role long enough, you internalize it. And if you are going to play a role, why not play your appealing, positive self instead of your negative, unattractive self?

Is that phony? No. We are all multi-faceted persons; we get to choose which of our facets we wish to display to the rest of the world. This is not phony. The positive facets are part of the real you too. You don't have to be a certain way just because you have always been that way. If being that way is not productive in your life, choose to display a more useful facet of yourself.

If your approach to life, to others, to yourself is not creating happiness in your life, dig in and discover some of your other facets. Savor and embrace each part of yourself. Then pick the facets you want to show. The negative ones — yes, they are part of you too, part of what makes you a human being — should be savored and cherished also. Cherish them as part of your bond with the human condition. Use them to enhance your compassion for others. Then, put them aside, knowing they are a part of you — a part you choose not to display on a daily basis.

Accentuate the positive. Put your best foot forward. Put on a happy face. You've heard those comments before. They aren't just platitudes. They make sense. However, that doesn't mean you can't ever show your negative side. You do get depressed at times. You do experience episodes of anger and irritability simply because you are human. Just remember that you don't have to express any particular mood or characteristic every moment of your life — that would be phony. You are a constantly changing being and you are entitled to the full range of emotional reactions. However, if most of your life is lived on the less positive side, you are not going to be happy. Something needs to be changed and only you can change it.

Life is a confidence game. I don't know who said that first but I do know that it's true. Those with the most confidence are most often the winners in the game of life. The confident aren't always the most outgoing. Quiet, unassuming people can be secure and successful in social relationships, but the fact remains that you must make your presence known in the world. If you can do it quietly, good for you. Most of us need to make a little noise.

After my divorce, I was feeling a little unsettled and cautious about getting back into dating. And like everyone who has been "off the market" for a while, I was asking questions like "How will I meet men?" and "What if no one wants to date me?" I even had a short period of real doubt in which I commented to a friend that I was afraid that no one would want me. She told me to stop feeling sorry for myself and "get out there." She insisted that no one knew that I was available and, until they did, my attitude would only be creating self-fulfilling prophecies. I am very lucky to have friends who feel free to express such helpful information. Before you get angry with people for being honest with you during your low periods, try to evaluate the validity of their comments. It may provide the push you need to get moving again.

If no one knows that you are socially available, you can't expect to be included in activities and events. So you must approach the world openly and confidently with an expectation of success in whatever direction you choose.

What kind of confidence do you need? Confidence in yourself and in your abilities, especially the ability to be accepted by others as the person you are. It's called self-confidence and at its base is a belief that you are an acceptable person. You must like and accept you. You must be aware of your strong points and take pride in them.

The confidence you have in yourself, or the lack of it, is expressed in everything you do and say. Do you speak with conviction or do you mumble? Do you stand tall and look people in the eye when you talk? Do you dress to please yourself or to please others? Can you laugh openly at your own mistakes or flaws? Can you calmly say thank you when you receive a compliment instead of feeling flustered and making excuses or belittling the comment? You know, someone tells you that you prepared a wonderful dinner and you say it was nothing. Of course it was something. Say thank you and smile.

Everyone feels a little insecure at times. Everyone gets a little nervous in new situations. Confident people, however, don't dwell on it. They feel that they belong wherever they are and act accordingly. If you have trouble doing this, let me give you a way to approach such situations. Ask yourself what is the worst thing that could happen in this situation. Figure out a way to handle that possibility. Once you have done that, nothing can happen that you can't handle. Chances are that the worst possible thing won't happen so anything less tense or embarrassing should be easy to deal with.

Whether it's answering a personals ad or going to a party where you won't know anyone other than the hostess, acting with confidence will help others to respond more positively to you. Most people will accept the impression of you that you give. So confidently express your positive self and enjoy the positive reactions of others.

It's up to you. You can do nothing and hope that something exciting will magically happen. Or you can step into the world and choose to have a more active and enjoyable life.

You are responsible for your own life. Once you accept this fact, the way you live your life will change. You will begin to live it for you in a way that will make you happy.

If you are past the teen years, it is no longer your parents "fault" that you are the way you are. You don't have to be a certain way just because people have told you that's what you are like or because you have always been that way. If you don't like the way you were raised and feel that it affected you negatively, get some therapy and change the messages from the past. All of that emotional baggage is probably weighing you down and keeping you from enjoying life fully.

Yes, we are products of our personal history. All that we have experienced has contributed to the development of the person we face in the mirror each day. But you can use that history to help you become the person you really want to see staring back at you. Just because your mother didn't see you as pretty doesn't mean that you are unattractive. Her perception was based on her standard of beauty. Create your own standard of beauty. This can't be done overnight, but you can start today. When you find yourself listening to the messages of the past or having negative thoughts about you, stop yourself. Replace the thought or message with one that is more positive. When you no longer reinforce the negative messages, their effect on your attitudes and actions will be lessened. This will allow you to more fully and freely express the confident you.

Believe in yourself. Don't pretend the messages of the past aren't there, just reevaluate them. If the old messages aren't valid, ignore them. Your judgments of you are the only worthwhile ones. Build upon your positives instead of focusing on the negatives that interfere with your image of you.

Do you sometimes feel the need for an instruction manual for you own life? Many people do. Life is a trial-and-error event. Instead of viewing this living-by-doing as a negative, as just one more chore to complete as you muddle through each day, why not view it as an opportunity to explore the very nature of yourself. Every experience you have gives you an opportunity for learning and growth. Each one allows you to practice being the person you are and to learn lessons that will allow you to be more successful in future situations. Each moment that you live fully and freely provides you with the motivation to continue living life in a way that is satisfying to you. The only real failure is not trying.

Approach your life as an adventure because that's what it is. This approach can make even the most mundane experiences enriching and enjoyable. If you think your life is dull, it may be because you are allowing it to be that way. Again, attitude is everything.

Let me give you an example of the difference attitude can make. I try to walk at least two miles every day. When time and weather permit, I walk four or more miles. Walking provides exercise and keeps my legs shapely. I could approach my walk as a chore, but that would make it boring and unpleasant instead of something to be looked forward to. I see it as a chance to think about a variety of topics and to fantasize about upcoming events in my life. It's also a chance to listen to the birds sing and to feel the breeze or the warmth of the sun. When I walk in my neighborhood, I see people I know and it gives me an opportunity to say hello, and it reinforces my sense of belonging in the community. With this approach, the walk contributes significantly to the enjoyment of each day. Remember, the only difference between play, work and drudgery is our attitude toward the activity in question.

By making some attitude adjustments, you can get control of your life. You are the person making the choices. You get to choose what you do, how you will approach activities, who is in your life, how you will relate to them, how much time you will spend with others and how much time you will spend alone. When you see yourself as a "chooser" instead of a "reactor," the day-to-day experiences of living become opportunities to partake fully in the adventure of your own existence.

Chapter 3
DECISION MAKING

Becoming a chooser for your own happiness requires a good system for decision making. Good decision-makers tend to have smoother sailing at all times. Philosophically speaking, life is a series of choices. If one makes good choices, one has a good life. If one makes poor choices, the chances for success and happiness are significantly reduced. If you frequently find yourself saying, "I wish I had done such-and-so" or "I shouldn't have done that," you may need to improve your decision-making skills.

How do you know if you have made a good decision? There are three ways to tell: (1) your choice of action actually solved the problem, resolved the situation, accomplished the goal or whatever according to the decision being made; (2) your choice did not create further problems; and most importantly, (3) you feel good about your choice.

Let's look at each of these. If you are short of money and you borrow on your charge cards creating new debt, did you really solve the problem? No. If you are angry with a friend and you choose to call her and say nasty things, are you less angry? Probably not. If, on the other hand, you approached each situation with the anticipation of a clear and desirable outcome, your choices would be more productive. Regardless of the situation, ask yourself what the best possible outcome could be. Then develop a strategy to achieve it.

In each of the previous examples, not only was the solution temporary or non-existent, each created new problems. You probably wouldn't feel very good about the outcome of such decisions either. All three tests of a good decision were failed. If, in the first example, you reviewed your total financial picture and decided to cut back on expenses for a while or to make a budget you could live with, you would probably pass all three tests. In the second example, if you calmly expressed your feelings instead of blowing up and saying nasty things to your friend, a resolution of the disagreement might be possible.

Again, it's a matter of choices. There are a variety of ways to handle all of life's hassles. The best part of any situation is that you get to make choices about how you live your life. I know that you may be thinking, "Sometimes, I have no choice." Not true. You always have choices. What you may really be saying is that you don't like the choices you have.

For example, you want a new dress for an event but you know that you aren't able to fit it into your budget right now. You can choose not to buy. You can shop your closet instead or borrow a dress from a friend or, if you really can't face going in an "old" dress, don't go at all.

Get creative. There are always a lot of choices. Stretch your mind and see what you can come up with. Give yourself time to review the situation and create options. Unless a situation involves life and death, most decision-making situations allow time for thinking. Remember that very few of the decisions that we make have lasting significance. In the course of your life, most of them will have little or no impact. We really don't make very many big decisions. Marriage and career are the only really big decisions and even those can be changed. All the rest seem to be related to those two.

So how can you learn to make good decisions? There is a seven-step process that will accomplish it fairly easily. With practice, the seven steps become almost automatic, but in the beginning, you may have to take the time to do each one systematically.

Step One: Define the situation, problem, issue, whatever. Determine what for you would be a desirable outcome. This is the hard step. If you mess up here, the rest of the steps won't help. For instance, if you are continually sniping back and forth with a friend, maybe what you need is not a new friend, but reassurance of your importance in this person's life. If you sit at home all the time, maybe the problem is not that you have no friends, but that you are afraid to let yourself get fully involved with them. Maybe you are afraid that you won't find a husband if you enjoy being single too much. If you feel that you don't have enough money, maybe the problem is not the number of dollars you have or don't have, but the way you handle them.

Sometimes this step is not complicated at all. You simply have to choose between two alternatives like whether to go to Hawaii or to the Bahamas for vacation.

Whatever you are dealing with, make sure the problem is clear in your mind and that you have some idea of what you want in the end. You have to ask the right questions to get the right answers. Even then, there may be some cases where there are no right or wrong answers, only acceptable alternatives.

Don't make your objective too large. "I want to be happy all the time" is an unrealistic goal. Break it down. Make it more attainable. For instance, "I'm not happy with my life the way it is. What are some things I could do to make life more satisfying on a daily basis?"

Step Two: List the alternatives available to you. Get really creative here. List even the ideas that seem stupid. This is not the time for evaluation. This is the time to let yourself see that you do have choices. Within those stupid options, there may be the seed of a possible solution.

Step Three: Gather information and review your resources. Whether it's reading *Consumer Reports* or talking to a friend, another opinion or piece of information can't hurt. Maybe you need to visit some stores or car dealerships to compare prices. Or review your budget to see how much money you actually have available. Until you complete this step, you won't really know which of your alternatives are viable. Give this step all the time it needs.

Step Four: Evaluate your alternatives. This is where you begin to eliminate alternatives. If you really don't have the money to buy a new car, doing so is not a workable alternative. You can now put more consideration into buying a used one or fixing your old one. If you really can't stomach singles dances, this is not an option you will find useful for meeting members of the opposite sex.

As you evaluate the alternatives, you will discard some because they are unrealistic in light of the information you have and the resources available to you. Eventually you will be left with a couple of possibles. Use the next step to choose between them.

Step Five: Pick the best one. You can do this by applying the three criteria for good decision-making. Ask yourself the following questions. Will this alternative actually resolve the dilemma or achieve the goal? Will it create new problems? How do I feel about it?

Step Six: Live with it. Walk away from the decision-making situation for a while, then ask yourself the three questions again. If the answers are satisfactory, go on to step seven.

There is one caution you must follow during step six. Put aside negative thinking and worrying. Neither is productive. Both are a very big waste of precious time and emotional energy.

Step Seven: Act. You must implement your decision. Otherwise, you accomplished nothing and are no closer to resolving your dilemma or achieving your goal. If you have difficulty getting started, sit down and actually write out a plan of action. Then do it. If it's something simple but unpleasant that you must do, set a deadline for completing the unpleasant task and follow through. Perhaps you can even make the unpleasant task easier to do by breaking it down into smaller, more pleasant tasks.

Remember that we frequently make decisions by doing nothing. In fact, some people make most of their decisions in this way so that they don't have to take responsibility for the outcomes. If you do nothing when action is required, you have still made a decision. You decided to do nothing. In some cases, that's okay. It may be the alternative of choice. In most cases, it's not okay. It becomes a matter of who's controlling your life — you or some esoteric external force. If you choose to "let the chips fall where they may," you have no cause for complaint when things don't turn out the way you would have liked them to.

This seven-step process works. However, it takes practice. The more you do it, the better you get at doing it. We learn to make good big decisions by making good small decisions.

You can use this process not only to solve problems and make decisions, but to improve the quality of your personal and social life. The seven steps allow you to avoid the negative "I can'ts." If you put your mind to it, you can do almost anything. Luck has little to do with it. Chance favors a prepared mind. If you are truly looking for a way to do something, you will find it. If you are open to possibilities, regardless of the issue, you will find opportunities for positive outcomes. In such cases, you create your own luck.

What if you go through all of the steps and still do not end up with the desired outcome? Or what if you find out later that you actually made a mistake? So what? Forgive yourself for being human and do what you can to rectify the situation. Then go on from there. This is not the first mistake you have ever made and it probably won't be your last. View it as a learning experience and make it count for something. Next time you will do it differently. And remember, unless someone dies, anything can be fixed.

This is a book about choices. Good choices create a happier and more satisfying lifestyle for you and those close to you. You have now been given a system for making choices which, along with your positive attitude about yourself as a single person, you can take with you as you move into the chapters which deal with your relationships with others.

However, there is still one area we must address before looking at those relationships. The next chapter deals with the hassles of life that we use as excuses for not living life fully. If you continually find yourself wandering from crisis to crisis, you have neither the time nor the energy for enjoyment. It's quite possible that you may be creating these crises as a way of sabotaging your acceptance and enjoyment of your life as a single person. "See, if I were married, life wouldn't be so hard. There would be someone there to help me." There is someone there — *you*! The next chapter may help you to discover the strengths that you already possess.

Chapter 4
HASSLE FREE LIVING

Life is not fair. Stuff happens. We can't deny the fact that life presents a multitude of hassles on a daily basis. Hassles, whether large or small, create stress. You may not be able to avoid all of the hassles, but you can limit their effects.

Some of the hassles and the resulting stresses can be controlled; some cannot. The secret to enjoying life is to take control of the ones you can so that you won't be overwhelmed by the ones you can't. Let's look at some of the more common stress producers and examine the level of control you can have.

Work. Do you like your job? Nearly half of the American work force does not. If you don't like your job, why are you doing it? And what is it about your job that you don't like? Is it the people you work with, the boss you have, the work environment, the work itself? If your job keeps you in a constant state of turmoil, if you have to force yourself to go to work everyday, if you live only for vacations and "sick days," maybe you need to look for a new line of work.

What is it you really want to do? You don't know? Try this — what do you do that you really enjoy when the time is your own? What are your hobbies? What are your fantasies? If, for instance, you spend your time reading, editing might provide you with a new career direction. If you enjoy meeting and talking to people and if people respond positively to you, maybe sales is the answer. If you love clothes and have a flair for dressing, maybe fashion coordination is the field for you.

Think! We have all heard the old adage that says if you find a job you really like, you'll never have to work. What could you do to earn money that would make you happy, that would bring you more satisfaction than you are now getting from your job?

How did you get the job you now have? Many people "accidentally" ended up in the jobs they hate. Even those with college and technical training may have accepted a job following that training just to get a foot in the door. Unfortunately they took the rest of the body with them and got locked into the "golden handcuffs." Now a job change may mean a reduction of income and benefits. It involves major risks. The new position may lack security. Will you have a job tomorrow? Next year? The fear of being without a job promotes the idea that you'd better stay where you are whether you like it or not. Major stress results.

If it's a problem with the boss, perhaps a switch to a different department, a different office, or a different employer may take care of it. But before you take these steps, ask what you don't like about this boss. Does he or she ride you, criticize you, hold you back? Is it a personality conflict? Maybe it's you — do you do quality work? Are you continually complaining or negative about everything?

Are co-workers your problem? Can you find a way to deal with them? If not, can you avoid the most irritating of them?

The key here is to spend some concentrated time identifying, then dealing with or removing the hassle, even if it means changing jobs or changing employers. Put some real thought into it. Make plans and check out the territory before making a change. Move carefully, but *move*! Whether that means a change in the way you approach your work, a change in the work itself or a change in the work place, change is required. Complaining won't make a difference. Action will. Take control. Don't let your personal power — your energy for life enjoyment — be sapped in a struggle to tolerate a situation which has become intolerable to you.

Undependable Inanimate Objects. "If it ain't broke, don't fix it," or "fix it before it gets worse." We all walk a fine line when it comes to the objects we depend upon. Not only do we have to deal with the frustration caused by their malfunctions, we have to find the time and money to do the repairs or to buy new ones.

So what do you do? Make a judgment call. Which presents mere inconvenience? Which could lead to real disaster? Make your decision and accept the consequences.

If I hear a noise in the engine of my car, I probably should deal with it now instead of complaining when the car dies during the rush hour on the expressway. If, however, the ceiling light bulb in the same car burns out, I can probably wait a while to fix it. I can pick a convenient time. If the toilet is overflowing, fix it now. If the faucet has a slight drip, well? Each person has to make a judgment call. That is not the same as ignoring the problem. When you note a problem and make a judgment, you are in control. When you ignore the problem, you are not.

If you have difficulty making decisions in these situations, ask yourself this question. If I don't fix this now, will I be creating greater problems for myself? Your yes or no answer should be your guide.

Time. Many of us consider time, or the lack of it, to be the greatest stress producer. Remember, time is relative. Make it work for you. How much of what you do really needs to be done? Are your standards too high? Haven't you learned to say no? Are you doing tasks that should have been done by someone else? Are you afraid people won't like you if you take time for yourself? Do you feel exhausted by your own life? Are you getting enough sleep? Do you have other resources that you could use to get more time?

You have heard the saying, "if you want something done, ask a busy person to do it." That's because busy people tend to be well-organized and don't waste time with little things that have little importance.

Take some time *today* to write down everything you did during this day. Then go through the listed items and ask the questions below.

1. **Did this really need to be done?** Why? If you can't give a reason, why did you do it? Was it part of the image you have of yourself as a person who does such things? Maybe the image is no longer appropriate or productive.
2. **Did you do this because it was important to you or because someone else expected it of you?** Would you have done it if it was totally up to you? If your answer is no, reevaluate such activities. I am not talking about your daily employment, although

you may have some options for better time use there as well. If it wasn't your task and held no value for you, why did you do it?
3. **What would happen if you said no to this activity?** Probably nothing. If you are already overwhelmed with work and play, don't be afraid to say so. Practice saying no. You have that right and should not burden your schedule with other people's tasks.
4. **Could you have done this more efficiently?** Did you really have to drive to the store, only to find they didn't have what you needed? Could you have called first?
5. **Would better planning have saved some time?** Could you have called for the tickets a week ago instead of having to buy them on your lunch hour today? Could you have bought the shoes for the outfit when you bought the dress?
6. **Could you have gotten someone else to do it?** Are you afraid to ask for help? Don't be. One December, after a car accident and a hospital stay for illness, I very boldly asked all of my friends what they could do to get me ready for Christmas. Everyone volunteered to do something and I had a wonderful Christmas. That taught me something. We all do favors and the ones we ask for are no different than the ones we volunteer for. In a two-way relationship, it balances out. If you are not in two-way relationships, make some new friends who will help, not hurt your life.

7. **Did you dovetail when possible?** Did you make a pile of things to copy or run to the copy machine every time you had one piece? Did you make a list of errands to be done and then do them in sequence of places and convenience or make six trips out of the way? Did you jot lists or write plans for other things while you were waiting on hold or standing in line? Did you do a load of laundry while cooking dinner?

   Most of us have enough brain power to do more than one thing at a time or to at least mesh activities. I seldom just watch TV. I pay bills or write letters or do the crossword puzzle. Most shows on TV do not require one's complete and undivided attention so it's a good time to do odds and ends.

8. **Could you hire someone to do this?** We are in the age of the personal service industry. There are people who will do almost anything for a fee — mow your lawn, do your laundry, shopping, house cleaning. (We will discuss money next, so don't start worrying about that yet.)

   Consider your personal preferences on this one. If you truly enjoy an activity and it brings you pleasure or relaxation in some form, do it. If you truly hate doing an activity, consider having it done for a reasonable price. Example — I enjoy painting walls; I hate house work. I would never hire a professional painter, but I believe cleaning people are worth every penny they charge.

9. **Did you get enough sleep in this twenty-four-hour period?** Sometimes we feel overwhelmed by our

schedules just because we are tired. When we are overly tired, we are also less efficient so it's important to build in time for an adequate amount of sleep. When we are well rested, most of life seems to go better.

10. **Did you have any time just for you — for whatever you wanted to do?** Call a friend, read a magazine, take a walk, anything just for the pure pleasure of it. Taking care of you is probably the best way to make yourself feel less stressed by an overly busy schedule.

Now, some other suggestions for making better use of the limited time you have. Select stores that usually have what you want. If you have the time, you can then browse in other stores, but if you are shopping for specific items, go where you know you can get them. Try to find stores where check-out time is reduced. Standing in line is a very big waste of time unless you use it to do other things such as noted in item seven in the preceding list.

Reevaluate your standards. Unless you have six little kids or are extremely messy all by yourself, your home will not need to be cleaned every week. A half-hour touch up should make it presentable if you are having company you want to impress. Microwave isn't the same as homemade, but it sure saves time. Think about it for a while. I'll bet there are tasks you could eliminate completely from your schedule. The time you free up could bring you much pleasure and satisfaction.

Time is one of your most valuable resources. Make it work for you. Each day can and should bring you relaxation and pleasure. Some of this is attitude. Once you have eliminated the pointless activities and those you were doing for others that they could have done for themselves, watch your approach to activities. Are you creating stress by continually thinking that you can't possibly get everything you need to do done? Does this stress lead you to procrastinate, thereby doing the same task mentally a number of times instead of once in actuality?

Think about what you are doing now and, if it seems that there are too many things to do, slow time down. Breathe deeply and give yourself affirmations that say, "I will get everything done today that really needs to be done. If I don't, the world will not come to an end." Do what you can, take some time for yourself and let the rest go. In the course of your life, it will probably make no difference.

Money. Worry about money is one of the more stressful things that single women have to concern themselves with. I am not going to try to tell you how to spend your money. If you truly don't have enough money to cover basic expenses like food, clothing and shelter, I can't help you. Maybe you need a better paying job or help to collect child support or a credit counselor. If it's a matter of poor money management skills, get a book on budgeting or take a class in family finance.

What I do have to offer is a number of suggestions for ways to afford the things you want on a less-than-generous budget. If you have plenty of money, skip ahead to the next section. If not, read on.

First of all, check out your attitude about money. What does it mean to you? What is it for? Do you need it for security? Is it part of your self-image? Or is it just a means to an end — something that allows you to have enjoyment in your life.

Nearly twenty years ago, one of my sisters told me she was tired of hearing me "talk poor." She said she didn't want to hear anymore of the "I can't afford it" stuff from me. She said I was poor because I thought poor. After I got through feeling sorry for myself and being angry with her, I gave her comments some real thought and it surprised me to find that she was right. My mentality about money said that I was not able to have and do the things I wanted because I didn't have a large income. Well, my income since then has barely kept pace with inflation and yet I have just about everything I want and have been able to have many things just for fun. I paid my son's way through college. I've taken two trips to Europe, traveled to a number of major cities in the U.S., seen all the plays, sporting events and concerts that I've wanted to see. I have a closet full of clothes and own my own home filled with furniture and furnishings that I enjoy.

What changed? Not my income level but my attitude. Instead of immediately thinking "I can't afford it," I started saying, "I'll bet I can find a way." The way has developed into a pattern for me which includes only two steps — first prioritize, then economize.

Prioritize. What do you really want from your discretionary money? That's the money you have left over after essential expenses like food, shelter, utilities and transportation. It does not include credit card payments on unpaid balances which you carry from month-to-month. Get rid of those as soon as possible and become a cash spender with a habit of paying any credit card usage in full each month. Those unpaid credit card balances may be the reason you have no discretionary money.

What's important to you? A fabulous wardrobe? Travel? A well-decorated house, apartment or condo in a prestigious area? Which is most important to you and when will you have "enough?" At what point will you have your home the way you want it? Do you need a new wardrobe every season? Must you always have the latest styles? Are you satisfied as long as you have something to wear for every occasion? Does it bother you to be seen in the same outfit more than once?

This is a matter of values. And it's also one that involves other factors such as time. Do you value a clean house, but have no time to clean it yourself? Perhaps you will give priority to hiring a cleaning person. Choices must be made. They will be easier to make if you identify what is really important to you in the scheme of things.

I can give examples from my own life. I like clothes but I don't like shopping. So as long as I have something appropriate to wear for every possible occasion, I'm happy. I buy items I like and take good care of them so that I'm prepared to go anywhere, anytime. I'd rather spend my money on entertainment and social activity. I'd like to do more foreign travel but know that I must be willing to save and plan ahead for expensive trips. For now, in addition to the travel involved with my job, I plan short trips to closer places where I can have a good time for a small expense. I value my time so I choose to work only part-time so that I can be free to do things during the week as well as on weekends. When I was teaching full time, I chose not to work during the summer for similar reasons. Having such values clearly in mind makes it easier for me to make choices about saving and spending money.

Economize. This means one must find a way to pay less than full price, not that one should compromise quality or settle for something other than what was desired.

Shop sales. My favorite price is second markdown. Most stores are selling 50-75% off long before the end of each season so they can make room for new merchandise. July and August are great months to buy summer clothes. You get them at rock-bottom prices and can wear them for the rest of the warm weather season and use them to begin the next warm season in style. January through March is the best time to buy winter wear for the same reason. Or go to the multitude of discount stores and outlet malls that have popped up everywhere and buy on sale during any season. All of this requires planning ahead, but it works. You can be well-dressed on a budget.

If you love to travel and give it a high priority, watch for bargain fares, collect miles with the airlines or with a co-branded credit card that gives miles with an airline. Do whatever you have to do to reduce costs. There are many ways to travel inexpensively. Do you have to stay at the best hotel in town? As long as the room is clean and you get fresh sheets and towels, who are you impressing by paying $200.00 a night instead of $50.00?

Buy an entertainment book for the largest city near where you live. The approximately $35.00 you spend will be minimal compared to the savings you get in one-half off or two-for-one coupons for theater tickets, sporting events, dinners, even car washes. Buy season's tickets. They usually cost less and have some extra benefits in terms of invitations to special events. If you love theater, try the local university productions. Tickets are usually $10-15 instead of $25-75 per person.

Use other people's things. Clothes, party supplies, lawn furniture, anything you need occasionally can be borrowed from close friends. Barter. Prior to buying a condo, I owned a house with a yard. I had no garage; I stored items like my lawn mower, ladders and bicycle in my neighbor's garage instead of buying a storage building for my back yard. Once a year, I cleaned the garage or mowed her lawn or raked her leaves. We were both satisfied that we had a fair deal. Prioritize, then economize. Use your resources to bring you a more satisfying existence.

Children. Yes, children are stress producers. Ask any single mother about this one and she will be able to tell you that they take time, energy, commitment, money and some of just about every resource she has. Hopefully, she will also tell you they bring her a lot of joy and satisfaction.

I will not try to tell you how to parent your children. There are literally hundreds of books available for that. What I will do is offer suggestions for reducing the hassles with children that produce stress.

1. **Mean what you say.** Make statements of potential consequences and follow through. Empty threats get you nowhere. For example: Not eating dinner leads to no dessert. Not getting a job means no car use. Homework not completed means the TV remains off until it's done. You are the adult. Act like it. Set fair rules and stick to them. An argument with a preschooler is an exercise in futility. Slapping your teen will only cause resentment.

2. **Let your kids help.** They are members of the family unit and should contribute to its success. Any child who can walk can pick up after himself. Each age gives a child new abilities that should be used to ease your load. You are a parent, not a slave. Work with your children to determine their preferences. For instance, train them to do laundry when they reach an age where they start caring about clothes.
3. **Show your children love every day.** It builds self-esteem. Kids who feel good about themselves behave better and demand less.
4. **Allow your children to learn self-comforting and self-entertainment skills.** This starts in the crib and is essential for a lifetime.
5. **Satisfy their needs for attention when they need it.** If you give a kid thirty minutes to an hour of undivided attention when he or she needs it, the rest of the day will belong to you. This is true regardless of age.
6. **Make some time for you.** Every day. Even a four-year-old can understand "mommy needs some quiet time." Claim the hour after their bedtime as an hour to pamper you.
7. **If you talk to them when they're little, they'll talk to you when they're big.** Establish good communication at an early age. It will pay off in the teen years.
8. **Remember that kids are people too.** Respect their rights as human beings and show them the same courtesy you would an adult. You will get respect and courtesy in return.

9. **Enjoy them.** Kids can be great fun.
10. **Don't try to do it alone.** Make friends with other parents and develop child care arrangements, toy and clothing exchanges or whatever else you can agree on that will save time and money. If you have young children, get a reliable sitter who loves your kids and enjoys spending time with them. When you find one or two, keep them around with courtesy and good pay.

What about their dad? If he's still in the picture, allow yourself to thoroughly enjoy the breaks the weekend visitations give you. If this creates hassles because you and he are into power games and get into arguments, see a counselor. You are an adult. You can't change him — you tried, remember? But you can learn some more productive ways of dealing with him. Get control of you and many of the hassles with him will stop. Don't let his behaviors turn you into a monster.

You can choose to remove the hassles from your life. I hope the questions and suggestions in this chapter have given you information that will help you to make some better choices for yourself. It will take practice, but you can take control of your life.

If you find that you are unconsciously holding on to the hassles to keep yourself from moving forward and getting more happiness for yourself, perhaps you need some professional counseling to get you back on track and moving again. Don't be afraid to seek help. Keep in mind the fact that if you get rid of the major stress producers, the stress will go with them. Then you will find the little hassles easier to live with.

The benefits of reduced stress will include a stronger sense of who you are and what you can do. Not only will you be more relaxed, but you may begin to like yourself and find more enjoyment in your lifestyle.

With the additional time and energy you free up by removing the hassles, you can create a fuller social life for yourself. The next chapter will help you to make positive choices as you open yourself to a wider range of personal possibilities.

Chapter 5
THE FINE ART OF SOCIALIZING

How do you judge your social success? Is it by the number of phone calls you receive? The number of party and social event invitations you get? The number of dates you have? The number of members of the opposite sex who seem to want to know you? The busyness of your life?

If you are evaluating your social success by the numbers, how many is enough? None of the answers to the above questions is a valid measure of social success. The only realistic and valid measure of social success is how well received you are by others and how YOU feel about it.

If the phone seldom rings, if no one invites you out, if you haven't been on a date in months, does that make you a social failure? Are you, therefore, a reject? Absolutely not! As long as people respond positively to you when you do make attempts at interaction, you are still socially successful. As long as you enjoy spending time with the person who provides the most stable and ongoing relationship in your life — *you* — then you can't be a social failure. If you like yourself, you are always in good company.

While the previous statement may seem oversimplified, it is nonetheless true. However, humans are social beings and most feel the need to have other people in their lives. Since this is a fact of life, let's look closely at your interpretations of social behaviors.

Why do you want to have friends? I know this seems like a stupid question, but it definitely is not. It is a very important question, the answer to which will determine how many friends you have and whether or not those friendships are satisfying to you. If we look at some of the answers, you will see what I mean and perhaps understand why we sometimes feel betrayed by the people we call friends.

Before we do that, let's talk about what people mean by friends. We tend to call everyone we know on an ongoing basis a friend. By friends, do you mean intimates? Do you mean people of the same sex only? The opposite sex only? Do you mean companions? A companion and a friend may be two different things. We may have companions who are also friends and we may have companions who are just that — people we spend time with and with whom we engage in some social activities. And we all know some people who are merely acquaintances, people we have met and socialized with at work, in the neighborhood or at social events. We enjoy knowing them but feel no need for an ongoing and involved connection.

The difference between acquaintances, companions and friends has to do with the level of involvement and the expectations we have of the people we include in each category. If you consider someone a friend and what you really have is a companion, you may be sadly disappointed.

Let me give you an example. I have a network of relationships with people who get together often for various activities and occasions. If I think of just ten of these people, three are probably friends, two are just acquaintances and five are companions. The two acquaintances are people I like and whose company I enjoy, but to whom I feel no ongoing allegiance, nor do they feel any toward me. We are friendly, can converse on a variety of topics and see each other at social events fairly often. The companions are people I see more often and will call if I want someone to go with me to an event. I do not feel obligated to invite them to every thing I do, nor do I feel any sense of obligation to do things with them on a regular basis. The three who are friends will be included in all of my group social activities. I will share the intimate details of my life with them. I trust them to keep my secrets and respect my feelings. I care about their feelings toward me and do what is required to maintain their friendship. I also feel hurt when I feel they have neglected to consider my feelings or if they ignore me.

The three who are my friends are not necessarily friends with each other. I have a close relationship with Carolyn, Marie and Michelle. They do not have a close relationship with each other. I am friends with Carolyn and Marie; they are companions with each other. Michelle is my friend, but she is an acquaintance to each of the others. This is all part of the dynamics of human relationships and it is important to define the dynamics so that we don't set up unrealistic expectations of others who are not involved with us in the same way we want to be involved with them. Recognizing the different levels of involvement saves a lot of hurt feelings and allows each of us to make decisions about behaviors and activities as separate and distinct individuals.

Many years ago, I heard a psychologist on a radio talk show say that he thought that anyone who said that she had more than three friends was probably kidding herself. A friendship takes time and energy and most of us do not have enough of either to maintain more than three ongoing close friendships. If one of those three is a roommate or lover, that only leaves room for one or two others.

The number of companions and acquaintances you have can be limitless depending on your life schedule and level of energy because you can adjust the amount of time and energy you spend on them. Friends have expectations; expectations that you will listen when they need to talk, that you will make time to see them, that you will include them in your life. That means we must choose our friends wisely so that we don't sap our own energy levels or short-change the friendship. Equal friendships — where each person contributes fully to the friendship — are usually the most lasting and satisfying. They do what close relationships should do. They enhance your existence.

Now, back to the original friendship question. What is it that you expect of friends and what will you give them in return? This is what's known as the economic theory of relationships. It requires a balance of costs and benefits. The costs are what you must give in order to get benefits from and to maintain the relationship. The benefits are the value the friendship has in your life. That is why this is such an important question. And the answers you give yourself may reveal a lot about you. You may discover that in some cases the costs are too great for the benefits received. You may find that some of these friendships are actually getting in the way of your own growth and it may be time to spend your resources of time and energy on more productive friendship choices.

Let's look at some of the reasons why people remain in nonproductive relationships.

Some people have friends to complain to. No, this is not a joke. Think about it for a minute. Have you ever known someone who only talks to you about the problems he or she is having? All the two of you do is share the down side — how terrible things are going at work, how badly the men or women in your life treat you, how little money you have, how nobody interesting is in your life, the awful thing someone else said to you. And if anything positive or exciting comes up, there is a lull in the conversation which gets broken by one or the other of you making negative predictions or comments about the positive or exciting activity.

Each of you has a vested interest in staying negative because that's the basis of your friendship. Should one of you actually begin to have a more positive life, the friendship will probably end. Why? Because you changed the rules. When this happens, can you maintain the friendship? Maybe. Try this. Start each conversation with something positive or joyful that is happening. You don't have to dwell on it, just mention it. Do this for four or five conversations. Then try interjecting more positives into the conversation each time you talk. If you find your friend becoming distant, keep trying but begin to evaluate what this friendship is doing to you. If the only way you can stay friends is to live on the negative side of life, it may be time to move on. Harsh as it may sound, your major responsibility is to you and your own growth and happiness.

You don't want to "abandon" your friend? Try to help him or her to become more positive. Ask him or her to tell you about the good things that are happening, saying that you need to hear about some happy things. Or add some laughter by relating a humorous incident that has occurred.

If your friend is not ready to move on and you are feeling some guilt, let me remind you that we each grow at our own pace. Your friend may not be ready to move on but, if you are, you must. You do not have to sacrifice yourself for your friend. Perhaps you can maintain a limited contact and encourage him or her through your example to grow into a more positive and happy person. The cost of remaining negative with him or her is too great a price to pay for friendship.

A final reminder — we all have negative periods; we all have times when we need to vent our frustrations. Having someone who will listen and empathize is one of the benefits of friendship. If that's what is happening with your friend, listen and keep encouraging the positive. Don't join the negative.

Some people have friends because they are afraid of being alone. Friends chosen out of this type of desperation are often people who do not present opportunities for growth in one's life. We may have little in common or even be treated with a lack of courtesy and respect in such relationships. Some people are willing to accept these relationships because they fear aloneness. They would rather be treated badly than be ignored.

If you don't want to be alone, make a point of meeting a variety of people. Check out the chapter on social networking. There are many people available to you who will share your interests and be willing to treat you with the courtesy and respect you deserve.

More importantly, you are not alone. *You have you!* If you like you and are your own best friend, you will be less likely to feel loneliness. Perhaps what you need are more acquaintances and companions, not friends who sap your energies. The world is populated with billions of people. You have a multitude of opportunities to know literally hundreds of them in a variety of relationships. You are cheating yourself if you settle for desperation "friendships."

Some people have friends to validate themselves. These are usually mutual-use friendships. Each person is receiving some benefits, or he or she would not stay in the relationship. Some people will only be friends with a certain type of person — a person they think others like and look up to because of factors like good looks, position or popularity. Or they choose people who they can feel better than — like the gorgeous woman who chooses a truly unattractive woman for a friend. The attractive woman might not even like or enjoy the unattractive one, but when she compares herself to her, she feels good. In this type of friendship each person is using the other. One gets to associate up; the other gets to feel better about herself. For each woman this friendship selection indicates an insecurity problem which needs to be addressed since it is probably creating difficulties in other areas of living as well.

Some people have friends so they will feel needed. The only role some people know how to play in relationships is the helper person so they choose needy people for friends. This may indicate a fear of abandonment — if someone needs me, he or she won't shut me out or ignore me.

While giving to others is commendable, it frequently leads to resentment and a feeling of being used. The helper person gives to others because it satisfies an image of herself as a good and worthy person. It is, however, easy for this type of relationship to get out of balance. When the giver finds herself in need, her friends may abandon her or appear to. Why? Again because the rules of the friendship changed and it is no longer possible for the relationship to continue without a change from each of the persons involved.

There is nothing wrong with helping others, but each of us needs to both give and get. We want to be needed but we also need at times. If the friendship is not a two-way relationship, feelings get hurt and the friendship ends. Both people feel betrayed.

Some people have friends so they won't have to be responsible for their own lives. Friends are just people to use as a sounding board for the latest crisis. They are there to help make decisions, or so it appears. In every situation, the person takes a poll by calling everyone she knows to ask what he or she thinks should be said or done in response to a certain event. This person knows what she wants to do to begin with but needs to involve others so she won't have to take the blame if things don't go well. This is an independence problem and one must confront it before one can have healthy, satisfying relationships with members of either sex.

Certainly it's appropriate to ask for the opinions of others when an important decision is being made, but if one has to consult more than one or two people, a problem involving independence and responsibility is evident.

Before closing the discussion on why people have friends, it is important to clearly identify a positive basis for friendship choices.

Some people have friends because they genuinely like people and they have developed their capacity to both give and receive. With this as a basis for friendship each person nourishes and is nourished. Both people give and get. Life is enhanced by the relationship. Life is fuller and more fun because of it. This is the healthiest and most productive basis for any relationship. The involvement is usually based on common interests and enjoyments. It usually involves a similar outlook on life and philosophy of living and includes an acceptance of and respect for individual differences. There is warmth and openness along with trust and respect which contributes to the growth of both parties in the friendship.

The most important point to remember from this discussion on friendships is that each of us gets to choose the people we share our life with. We also get to choose the level of involvement we have with each person. Since the choice is ours to make, doesn't it make sense to choose people who will contribute to the enjoyment of living and to our personal growth.

This examination of social relationships may be leaving you with a feeling that something important has been left out. The opposite sex? Not at all — we can and must have friends, companions and acquaintances of both sexes if we wish to have a fulfilling and well-rounded life. And, if your goal is to establish a lasting, loving relationship with a member of the opposite sex, a warm friendship may be the most significant facet of that relationship.

What you are probably missing in all of this is a sense of connectedness. An example from my life might provide some insight into this feeling. Years ago, I called my sister in tears. When she asked me what was wrong, I told her that I was lonely. She said, "What do you mean you're lonely? You know lots of people." Yes, I did know a lot of people, but I didn't feel connected to any of them. We all want to feel important to someone besides our parents, our kids and those people who are "supposed" to love us. We want someone to choose to care about us, to care whether we are happy or sad, whether we are dead or alive. And that's what I was missing. And perhaps that's what appears to be missing in this chapter on social success. The next few chapters will address this issue, particularly as it applies to being important to someone of the opposite sex.

Chapter 6
SOCIAL NETWORKING

Your life feels empty. Nothing exciting is happening. Everyone is having more fun than you. And why is that? You are responsible for your own day-to-day living. Are you sitting at home waiting for the magic to happen? It won't — you have to make it happen.

First, let's get the excuses out of the way. You don't have any money. There's not enough time. You're too shy. You don't know many people. Nothing ever works out anyway, so what's the use of trying? You can never think of anything interesting to talk about.

What a world you have created for yourself! If you keep believing those excuses, you can be unhappy forever. Is that what you want? No. Then do something about it. You are the only one who can. It sounds like you may be stuck in what I call the "Rainbow Syndrome," named for a quote from Margaret Atwood's book *Cat's Eye*. "I want embraces, tears, forgiveness. I want them to arrive by themselves, with no effort on my part, like rainbows." Instead of staying stuck, create some rainbows.

Create a fuller life for yourself by social networking. It is said that we are only six people away from anyone in the world. For a seemingly far-fetched example, let's use the Pope. I know my sister who knows a priest who travels frequently to Rome and has met the Pope.

He knows Vatican personnel who communicate with the Pope daily and, through them, he could get me an audience. I'm only four people away.

You can do this with anyone. Try it. I'll bet you will find that it's true. Now, if you are that close to famous people, shouldn't it be a simple matter to meet people closer to you in geographical distance. Like your neighbors, your co-workers, the people in line at the bank, at the grocery store, in the doctor's office. Oh yeah, you say. So that's where I'm going to find my new best friend? Absolutely! Where did you meet your current and former friends?

You already know your neighbors and co-workers and there is nobody in either group that you would be interested in knowing. I thought you wanted friends, acquaintances, and companions. Maybe what you mean is that you only want to populate your life with people who put forth a certain image. Or maybe you only want to meet members of the opposite sex.

If you really want to have a fuller, more interesting and socially active life, you need an attitude adjustment. Open yourself to the possibility that you can connect with a variety of people. You can learn from them and bring much joy to your day-to-day living through them. You may meet people who will be friends for life, including the man of your dreams, if that is your goal.

You may connect for only a few minutes. That's okay, too. That chance encounter in the grocery store may give you an opportunity to think about a new idea or way of looking at a situation. It will then be a "great moment" in your life. Additionally you can always initiate a conversation at a social event with, "I met this person in the grocery store and he or she said that . . ."

That's a part of social networking. You create a social network just like you do a business network. One person introduces you to another. You get pieces of information from everyone and use them in ways that make sense for you.

Just as your business acquaintance may invite you to lunch, your new social acquaintance may invite you to a party. One person leads to another and soon your world is full of people — some acquaintances, some companions, some friends.

Let's deal with the excuses that are holding you back, the ones that are keeping you from being an active participant in the adventure of your own life.

No money. Wealth is as much an attitude as it is green pieces of paper. It doesn't take money to be open and friendly. If you mean you can't afford tickets or the right clothes, those things can be handled. Suggestions for doing so were in Chapter 4.

Money is not the key. It doesn't cost anything to smile and say hello or good morning to another person.

No time. Time is relative. Einstein said so. We always have time for the things that we really want to do. Think about your life. Are you doing things just to keep busy and calling them necessary? Does your house really need to be cleaned every week? Do you have to do laundry just because it's Saturday? Will the world come to an end if you don't write that letter today? Could you get someone else to do some of what "needs" to be done? Again, we make time for the things that are important to us. (Go back to the chapter on hassles.)

You don't know anyone. Sure you do. People are everywhere. What kind of judgments are you applying to them? Aren't they well-dressed enough, good looking enough, rich enough, active enough or whatever for you? Maybe what you mean is that the people you know now are not the kind of people you really want to associate with. Then go where those people are. Or smile, say hello and meet people wherever you go.

You're shy. Does that mean you are afraid? Of what? That you will say or do something stupid? So what? Everyone does at times and it's okay. Perhaps rejection is what you fear. How can a person you don't know reject you? People can reject your gestures of friendliness, but how can they reject you? They don't even know you. Forget it and move on. The planet is populated with billions of people and you will miss the chance to meet others while you are focusing on this perceived rejection. Remember, that's all it is — a perception, your reaction to an event.

Why try, it won't work anyway. If you think you can't meet and enjoy people in a mutually satisfying way, you can't. You create your own reality. Perhaps it's time to put away the experiences of the past and create a new reality with the more positive attitude you now have about yourself.

But that's what always happens, so how can you believe otherwise? Your so-called friends abandon you, betray you, let you down. Maybe you are choosing the wrong people for friends or are choosing people for nonproductive reasons. The most common nonproductive reason is that we are used to things the way they are and change would be uncomfortable. Nobody dies from discomfort, so take some risks and choose to meet some people who will enrich your life with joy and laughter.

You don't have anything to talk about. Then it's time you developed yourself conversationally. Start truly listening to the conversations of others. What do they talk about? Anything and everything. It doesn't have to be a question and answer session. In fact, if it is, it's no longer a conversation, it's an interview.

Prepare yourself with a variety of topics. You have a mind that works; you form opinions and have reactions to daily events. Don't be afraid to bring up a topic and express your feelings about it. So what if others don't happen to agree with you? You are entitled to your own reactions and opinions and stating them not only gives you a chance to hear them and test their validity, but the reactions of others will cause you to think further about the topic. Soon you are engaged in a lively conversation. Remember that we are talking about conversations, not arguments. If a discussion becomes an argument, let the topic go. If you have a vested interest in being right, you are going to turn people off. It's only a conversation, not a courtroom drama with lives hanging in the balance. Move on to something else. It's not important to convince others of your position unless you are running for public office. You're not, are you? You are in the company of others for enjoyment. Keep it pleasant.

Where do you get your topics? Get in the habit of watching the news on TV or of reading the paper. There are hundreds of news items that can be discussed with others. When I read books or magazines, I mentally collect conversation ideas and save them for times when I am in social situations so that I always have things to talk about.

Join in on the topics that others bring up. Your fresh ideas and opinions may be of interest to them.

When you are in a one-on-one situation with a new person, the range of topics you can discuss is limitless. In addition, you have each other's lives and history to talk about. A former friend, who was 50 at the time, used to say, "I don't know what's wrong with young girls who say there is nothing to talk about on a first date. I don't understand what they mean. You're just getting to know this person. There are a million things to learn about each other." Needless to say, she was one of the most popular women I have ever known.

I know, you hate small talk. What's big talk? I don't know that difference. If you are enjoying the company of another person, it's just conversation. Not big talk, not small talk, just talk. If you are in a situation in which you don't want to be with a particular person, that's probably what you mean by small talk. You are attempting to force conversation when neither of you really wants to talk to the other at all. So be quiet. In some situations you might just say that you feel the need for some quiet time. That would be appropriate when you are in the beauty shop or on a train or waiting in line. If you are at a party or social event where people are expected to interact, just excuse yourself and find someone you really do want to talk with. You don't have to be rude. Just do it with as little fuss as possible.

You don't need clever one-liners or humorous stories to create a good conversation. An interesting conversation is interesting because it's interactive, not because it's witty. You don't have to be an entertainer.

Also, remember that listening is just as important as talking. It takes both to communicate. We need quiet people and good listeners. Without them, the heavy talkers of the world would be lost.

Are you okay once a conversation is underway but don't know how to get things started? The best advice I can give is to just start talking. Just get your mouth moving with coherent sounds coming out. It doesn't have to be clever, but it does have to get another person's attention.

That's easy if you already know a person, but what do you do if it's a complete stranger? The same thing. Just get your mouth moving with coherent sounds coming out. It's probably best to avoid the trite openings, but if you can do them with a wink and a smile, even the most overused lines might work. They will at least let the other person know that you are trying to start a conversation. Better yet, just say hello and introduce yourself with the offer of a warm and friendly handshake.

If you are only uncomfortable when you try to initiate conversation with men, practice on women. You can use many of the same openings. Or meet the women at a social event and let them introduce you to the men in the group. Or join a group of people with both men and women already engaged in conversation.

It is not difficult to be a social conversationalist. Practice will help. After a period of time, conversation with new people can be as easy as talking with old friends.

That's it, then. All of your excuses are gone. There is no reason to live a non-social life unless you choose to do so and find your aloneness satisfying.

Chapter 7
CREATING A SOCIAL NETWORK

Your attitude about yourself and toward others is positive and you are approaching the world with openness and confidence. You are ready to find new friends, companions and acquaintances. You will need some tools to get started. These tools include a pen or pencil, a purse-sized notepad and a pocket calendar which you will carry with you everywhere you go. How else will you be able to write down names and phone numbers or jot notes about upcoming events?

That's right — you are going to start collecting names and numbers. If you are lucky, you'll meet a lot of people with business cards and save yourself some effort, but don't be afraid to ask people for a way to get in touch with them. Yes, that includes men. Men have been asking for women's phone numbers ever since the telephone was invented. Isn't it time we gave ourselves permission to do the same? That doesn't mean you only ask men for numbers. Ask women, too. This is a process of including people in your life, not excluding them.

If you have business cards, make sure you always have some with you. If your job doesn't give you a reason for cards, or if you would rather your new acquaintances didn't contact you at work, create some personal calling cards. This is not a new idea. Calling cards have been around for a couple hundred years. The only difference between those of the past and the ones you will create and purchase for yourself is the telephone number that you include along with your name. You don't need to put an address on it or even a description of something you do — just your name and number will do. Please don't get cute. Keep the cards simple. You will have an opportunity to reveal your personal style as you get to know people better. If you have a post office box number, feel free to include an address, but do not put a home address on the card unless you are truly adventurous or truly stupid.

You are now fully prepared to begin meeting people. Where do you go to do it? Wherever you want. We are talking about meeting people — both men and women, young and old — so it could happen anywhere. Like the grocery store, at church, the library, at work, at the airport, on a plane or in the waiting room of the car repair shop.

If you are comfortable at singles events like dances or club meetings, this is a good place to meet friendly people you may want to contact at a later time. When you get invited to parties, meet people that you can include in your social network. Talk with them for a while — long enough to establish yourself in their memory so that you won't be a complete stranger in future contacts. Find out what they like to do, what you have in common, their availability to do things.

You will soon have a list of people you can call on to be party guests, to go to social events with you or just to talk. Don't hesitate to use it. If you call someone and the person seems less than positive in his or her response, forget it and go on to someone else. Little by little, you will expand your network.

This doesn't mean that you will include only single people in your world. Married people, as individuals or in couples, can enrich your world too. The bottom line for creating a social network is that you must talk to people. Speak to others wherever you are. Be open and friendly. Smile. Be receptive to the efforts that others make to have a conversation with you. Remember that no one will approach you if you look sullen or morose, nor will they respond positively to you if you speak without warmth or enthusiasm. Talk about each other. Talk about pleasant things. Talk about the situation you are in whether it's the grocery store, the bank line, the party or the play you've just seen. Just talk. If you establish a rapport and are interested in further contact, find a way to get it. Even if you don't want to get to know this person better, you will have had practice conversing with others and will gain confidence in yourself as a friendly, outgoing person.

Of course you should use common sense. If a person strikes you as weird, follow your instincts and exercise caution. Trust your own judgments about the amount of information you want to share. With practice, you will improve your "bullshit detection" skills and begin to make better judgments about which people to include as potential persons in your social network.

If you get a number from someone, but he or she seems a little hesitant about it, call once and see what happens. If the response on the telephone is reserved or evasive, cross the person off your list. If the person seems genuinely glad to hear from you, talk for a while and get to know him or her better. If you're really not sure how the person will respond, call at a time when you are sure you will get their answering machine and leave a message asking for a return call. If you get no call, you have a very clear response indicating that this person is not interested. And that's all the response means. This person is not interested in pursuing a relationship with you. You have not been rejected so don't waste any energy worrying about why he or she is not interested. Move on to other people and other things. It's no big deal.

Another way to meet people or to get to know people better is to throw a party. If you don't know people before the party, you certainly will afterwards. No, I'm not suggesting that you invite total strangers into your home. That would be naive and dangerous. It doesn't even have to be in your home. Have a block party and use the street or use the club house in your apartment complex. Start with your neighbors and have a getting-to-know-you party. I did that several years ago in the back yard of my house so that I could get to know the people on my street. I simply created a flyer inviting everyone to a patio party and delivered it to each house. Each household was asked to bring a dessert or beverage and to come between 2:00 and 4:00 p.m. on a Sunday. It was a great success. I also had a Christmas party and used the neighborhood newsletter to invite the single people in my neighborhood to get acquainted with each other. Twenty-three people, both men and women, came. It was delightful! I am still interacting with about a dozen of them.

Create or join a special interest group. Have a meeting at your house. If you are a runner, join a running group and invite members to come over after a running event. Start a book discussion group or join one and have the next meeting at your place. For a time, I belonged to a parapsychology group which met at my house several times. Not only were the meetings interesting and entertaining, they gave me a chance to practice my entertaining and social skills.

Practice is a key word in all of the discussions in this book, whether it's dating or entertaining, meeting or talking to people. The more you do it, the better you get at doing it.

Once you have created a social network, keep it alive. Do call the people you have met to do things with you. If you like movies, call someone and ask him or her to meet you at the theater. Or ask someone to go to a play with you. Each of you pays your own way in this circumstance. This is not a date; it is a social contact with someone you are developing a relationship with. However, this same technique can be used with members of the opposite sex for relationship development as well. The tricky part is to make sure each of you knows what it's all about. Otherwise, one or both of you may misunderstand the meaning of the activity and the possibility for friendship or more may be lost to both of you.

Be a doer. Start organizing group events such as a movie or theater party. See if you can get enough people together to get a group discount. After the movie or play, go back to your house or to a nearby restaurant to discuss what you have just seen. Or call some people to try a new restaurant with you. If your area has some unique places like a sing-a-long bar or bacchi ball or feather bowling alley, take advantage of it by making a reservation for eight to ten people and organizing a group just for fun. At Christmas, get some people together to go caroling and then invite them to your house for drinks and dessert.

Be a goer. As you meet more and more people, you will begin to get invitations to parties and activities. As you create parties and events, people will begin to issue return invitations. Go to these parties and events. You will meet more people there. Don't be afraid to borrow friends — every activity you attend will introduce you to new people who can then become your acquaintances, companions and friends. If you like them and they like you, collect names and numbers and invite them to the next activity you organize.

If you are uncomfortable giving parties and creating social events, a second alternative is to make friends with a social networker. Some people are good at creating such networks and others are not. Some are not ready to take the imagined risks. Some may live in situations which preclude entertaining. If you are not good at creating a social network, having a friend who is accomplishes the same goal for you. You get to meet lots of people, attend events you wouldn't otherwise, and create a richer social life for yourself in general.

If you do elect to become friends with a social networker, be sure to keep the relationship in balance. As a payback, you may want to take this person out for dinner or to the theater occasionally. Or make sure you remember him or her nicely at Christmas or on their birthday. In the end, it will all balance out.

I do not spend a lot of time concerning myself with fairness in my social network. If I enjoy another person's company, I really don't care if he or she invites me in return. The pleasure and enjoyment I get from knowing the person is enough. I don't keep a score sheet. As long as my guests are contributing members in the group in some way, their company is all that is needed to keep things in balance. I do eliminate people from the network if they say no three times. If I invite a person on three different occasions to do something and each time he or she is unavailable or says he or she will attend and then doesn't show up, I cross the person off the list. Yes, I do have a list. It includes names and numbers of people who enjoy social activities and are willing to be a part of a variety of group gatherings.

I quickly eliminate women who ask me whether or not there will be any interesting single men in the group. If someone does not have any interest in activities that have a purpose other than matchmaking, she probably will not contribute positively to the enjoyment of the group as a total.

Okay, you are willing to give it a try but you haven't organized a social event, dinner party or any other kind of party in a long time and you are out of practice. If you are nervous and uncomfortable with the idea, what you need to do is start small. Invite a married couple whose company you enjoy to come over for a drink. Serve wine and some simple refreshments and practice your conversational skills. Or invite two or three friends to have dinner at your home. Practice with easy menus. This will help you to gain confidence and get past your nervousness.

After you have staged a few small events successfully, you will be ready to have larger events. The following information will help you to proceed with confidence.

The three essential ingredients for a successful party are (1) a clean, comfortable environment, (2) refreshments, and (3) people.

A clean, comfortable environment means just that. Your home should not smell of anything offensive and there shouldn't be cobwebs, dirt or bugs in evidence. (A later chapter will address the impression you make through the place where you live.) If you have animals, make sure they are well behaved. If they are not, put them in the basement or kennel them. Recognize that some very pleasant and entertaining people have allergies or are tense around cats or dogs. Just because you love Fluffy or Rover doesn't mean that everyone else will.

Furniture arrangements should provide places for people to gather in groups. Adequate seating should be available. That doesn't mean a chair for every person, however, a majority of your guests should be able to sit at any given time. Folding chairs or cushions on the floor are acceptable.

Refreshments can be simple or elaborate depending on the amount of trouble, time and money you want to give to the event. You could have it catered or order carry-out like Chinese or pizza. You could serve just snacks or dessert. Or you could serve a complete dinner. A lot will depend upon the size of the group and the time of day. That's up to you and your budget. Another option is to ask people to bring food or beverages. Most people will offer to do so when you issue the invitation. Take them up on the offer and be clear about what you want them to bring. You set the menu and assign each person something. You should still be prepared with some back-up food of your own. I always make sure I have extra food and beverages available. If it doesn't get used at the party, I can find a way to use it later. It's better to have too much than too little. Sometimes, you may want to provide the food and have your guests bring the beverages. Or have them bring desserts.

Whatever you choose to do about food and drinks, plan it so that you don't have to spend the whole time in the kitchen. Your guests want to socialize with you, not just with each other. That's part of the reason they came to the party in the first place.

You definitely need people to have a party. How many depends on the kind of party you are having. Experiment with this a bit and you will begin to get a sense of how many are needed to make a successful group for various activities. A caroling party will probably need at least twelve people. Eight or ten is a good size for a birthday party which features dinner. A movie or theater party needs six or more people. A costume party needs at least twenty to be successful.

You don't have to know everyone that you invite well. In fact, parties that you host are a good time to invite some of the new people you have met. I would make certain, though, that at least two-thirds of the people know each other. Otherwise, it becomes a meeting, not a party, and you will get stressed out in your efforts to create a cohesiveness in the group. Invite a core group of supportive friends, companions and acquaintances along with the new people you want to get to know better.

Invite at least one really outgoing person. This is a must. A person like this can save an otherwise boring party. And let's face it, if this party is a flop, you will have difficulty getting people to come to another one.

Unless you plan to invite fifty or more people, avoid afternoon parties with open times. If you invite twenty people to a four o'clock-until-midnight barbecue, you could end up with no more than four people in attendance at any given time.

My experience has been that single people and couples do not mix well in party groups of twenty or less. They don't have enough in common.

Single people usually do not attend Saturday night parties. They are afraid to commit to your party because "they might get a date," so it's best to plan parties whose guests will be primarily single people for Fridays or Sundays.

If you are giving a party during a holiday season, invite people well in advance. The same is true if you need to get tickets or if there is someone you really want to have at the party. Telephone invitations are usually more successful than written ones unless your party is an annual event. If you send a written invitation, ask for RSVP's or make follow-up calls. It's too easy to put the written invitation aside. A telephone call usually gets the party noted on the person's calendar.

If you are not an experienced party giver, it may be helpful for you to have a theme for the party. The theme can be anything from Christmas to birthdays. It could be something frivolous like a "welcome spring" party, with everyone being asked to bring one of their favorite spring flowers to the party. The theme will at least get conversation started and, hopefully, the party will develop and sustain itself from there.

Having done all you can to create a successful party, relax. You set the tone for the party. If you aren't having a good time, no one else will either. You don't have to "entertain" people as such, but you do have to be enthusiastic and act genuinely glad to have all of your guests in your home.

Every party giver has a few moments of nervousness. Don't let it throw you. The most common worry is that no one will show up. That's not going to happen, so instead of dwelling on such a remote possibility, just decide that you will have a good time with whoever does come.

This reminder should not be necessary; however, it is a fact of life that some people may drink too much at your party. If so, be prepared to ask for their car keys, to call a cab, or if you know the person well and are comfortable with it, to offer him or her a bed for the night. If you have any doubt about a person's ability to drive, please don't let him or her do so.

Once you start initiating social events, you will start getting invited to more events. If you want to continue to be invited, you must be a good guest. Only good guests get invited again. Poor ones do not. The following rules may be helpful in developing your party behaviors.

1. **A good guest brings the party with her.** No one is obligated to entertain you. You don't have to be the center of attention or the life of the party, but you do have to contribute to the enjoyment of the event in some way.
2. **A good guest arrives on time.** Even the most experienced party giver gets a little unnerved when no one has arrived thirty minutes after the party was supposed to have begun. He or she may also not be ready for you if you arrive thirty minutes early.

3. **A good party guest doesn't invite others without permission.** Call and ask if it's okay to bring another person with you. In some cases, your host or hostess may welcome additional guests. If it's a dinner party, probably not. If it's something involving tickets with the party afterwards, your guest may be welcome to attend the party later but will not be able to go to the ticketed event. For any other kind of party, the answer will probably be an enthusiastic yes, but it is always best to ask.
4. **A good guest doesn't ask who else will be there.** Your host or hostess is inviting you. If you like him or her, you will probably like the other people at the party. Definitely do not ask if there will be single men there. If that's the only reason you would have for going, stay home or go to a singles bar. It's not your host or hostess's job to matchmaker for you.
5. **A good guest gives a believable reason for saying no to an invitation.** If you really can't or don't want to attend, make sure your reason for not attending makes sense. Don't create elaborate or involved excuses. Your reason should sound like a reason, not an excuse.
6. **A good guest is honest.** Don't say you will attend and then not show up. If your host or hostess is planning on twenty people and only six show up, the party will be a flop. Be definite. If you can't be sure because of something like getting a babysitter, give a definite day when you will call back. Otherwise, it looks as if you are waiting for something better to come your way.

7. **A good guest is pleasant.** No arguing or rudeness is allowed when you are in someone else's home. If you find another guest truly offensive, avoid that person.
8. **A good guest dresses appropriately.** If you are not sure how to dress for the occasion, ask.
9. **A good guest thanks the host or hostess before leaving.** It is also appropriate to call within a day or two or to send a note saying how much you enjoyed the party.
10. **A good guest stays a while.** Commit yourself. Unless it's an open house, you should be there for most of the party. Even an open house requires a minimum one-hour stay.

Your social life will increase significantly if you follow the suggestions in this chapter. In fact, you may find yourself busier than you want to be. Instead of a wallflower, you have become a social butterfly. Enjoy it, but don't forget to leave some time just for you and for the development of one-on-one relationships with people of the same sex and the opposite sex. A life of social frenzy can leave you feeling just as empty as a lack of social activity does.

Balance is the key word here. You do get to make the choices and there are times when it's not only okay, but necessary, to say no to events and activities. As with all of life, the choices you make should be satisfying to you.

Chapter 8
MARRIAGE AND MATING

"I want a man in my life, I just don't want him in my house." Great line — not mine. I am quoting a comedienne named Joy Behar. It's an appropriate comment for a discussion on marriage and mating because it seems to speak for a lot of today's single people, both male and female. While we have not ruled marriage out, we find the freedom and independence of our lives so satisfying that we have begun to ask not "When will I marry?" but "Do I really want to get married?" Yes, there is a desire for a male-female relationship but not one which involves twenty-four hours a day of sharing and decision making.

Is such a committed, part-time relationship possible? Many people hope so. I do know one couple that has managed to create this type of relationship. They have been "dating" for over forty years. They have traveled the world together, see each other regularly and are accepted as a couple in their social circle. They live separately but the bonds that exist between them are as solid as those of many long-term marriages.

So why do people get married? Let's look at some of the reasons and see if they make sense.

You're supposed to. Oh, really! Says who? Maybe you have bought into this myth and are creating a lot of misery for yourself in a desperate search for Mr. Perfect.

Or maybe you are hanging on to Mr. Not-So-Perfect in hopes that one day he will marry you. Or maybe you are messing up a perfectly satisfying relationship with pressure to marry. Why? Will marriage make your life better, more satisfying, less painful? No! Happy is within you. No one can create it for you. A spouse may give you cause to make happier choices for yourself. A spouse may allow you to fulfill a fantasy for yourself. A spouse cannot make you happy. Before you marry just to be married, take a careful look at the costs and benefits.

You're tired of everyone asking why you are not married. Would you rather they asked why you are divorced? Both are extremely rude questions. It's nobody's business. Think for a minute about why people ask. Is it because they are miserable and envy the freedom you have as a single person? Is it because you are sending out messages that say, "I'm a reject because no one wanted to marry me."

I truly believe that anyone can get married if they aren't too fussy. Of course those marriages don't usually last because they are based on needs for acceptance and conformity, not on a solid relationship between people who have the ability to commit and compromise. Marriage just to be married brings joy to no one.

So you'll have someone to do things with. Like what? How many truly socially active married couples do you know? A lot of married couples only go out on special occasions and spend the rest of their time not communicating with each other. Many of them bore each other to death and the only thing they discuss is which television programs to watch each evening. Worse yet, many spend hours fighting in a futile effort to find a way to relate to each other.

Did you forget that friends can be companions too? You don't have to be married to have companions. And being married doesn't guarantee that you will have the companionship you desire.

You're afraid you are getting too old and if you don't marry soon, no one will want you. When I was working on my graduate degree, I had a professor whose first marriage occurred when she was sixty-three years old. I know a retired school administrator who was widowed for many years and remarried after retiring at age sixty-five. So what's too old? As an alive, vibrant and satisfied person you will always be attractive. Friendly, open people attract others regardless of age.

You want legitimate children. So what's illegitimate? We lost that term years ago. Everyday, women are electing to have children without choosing to have a husband. Some even select a man to father the child and make it clear that they intend to raise the child alone. Others opt for artificial insemination or adoption.

You want to have children? Have them. They will be "legitimately yours."

You don't want to raise a child alone. Does being married guarantee that you won't have to? Haven't you been reading the papers — nine million children live in single parent homes. Death and divorce are fairly common experiences. You might even end up married to someone who says he wants children but keeps putting it off. You could find yourself married to someone who fathers children with limited involvement afterwards. No guarantees, remember.

You don't want to grow old alone. Again, have you been living under a rock? Remember death and divorce.

You think people feel sorry for you or see you as a reject. Are you a reject? Do you act like one? Do you give people a reason to feel sorry for you? Then why should they? Check yourself out. If you are living a vital, interesting life, more people will accept you — perhaps even envy you — than will feel sorry for you.

You are tired of supporting yourself. Wouldn't a second income be great? Then you could have all the material things you want without waiting. Get real. Material things don't bring happiness. You create your own happiness. It comes from inside of you.

If you really need more money, find a way to earn it. Spend some time thinking creatively. Maybe it's a simple matter of spending less. A second income is a pretty poor reason to tie the knot. The marriage may, in fact, turn into a series of knots that tie you up forever.

You want to have a regular, safe sex life. You don't have to be married for that. And haven't you ever heard of extra-marital affairs? Just being married is not a guarantee that you won't get any diseases. Nor does it promise that you will get frequent, satisfying sex. One of the major problems in marriage happens to be centered around the sex life of the couple.

Again, there is nothing wrong with marriage. There is, however, something wrong with marriage for the wrong reason. The only good reason to marry is because the two of you have a strong, loving relationship and are committed to work at success within the marriage. Marriage will enhance your already satisfying life. This takes two mature people who share the same goals and are able to communicate freely with each other. It is based on respect and trust which take time to develop and lots of nurturing to keep.

Before leaving this topic, let me share a few thoughts about the mind games we play with ourselves. If a person really wants to get married, it is easy to ignore all the signals that say, "Whoa, this is not going to work!" So while you are thinking rationally, review the warning signals suggested by Landis and Landis, well-known researchers and writers in the field of marriage and family living.

Danger Signals in a Relationship

1. **Quarreling — especially if there is a pattern to the quarrels.** This may indicate that each person's needs are not being met or that there are significant differences in basic beliefs or standards or that you have serious doubts about the relationship. It may indicate that one or both of you is afraid of closeness and commitment. It could mean many things, none of them good for a permanent relationship.

    All relationships have some conflicts, but quarrels that are frequent and continue to be about the same issues are definitely an indication that something is not right in this relationship. Be especially careful if the fights involve personal attacks or the use of "if you loved me" statements.
2. **Some subjects cannot be discussed.** In this case, it's not just differences that are indicated, but an inability to handle the differences in a compromising way. It may indicate a basic lack of respect for the other person's approach to living, an effort to control the other or a lack of adaptability on the part of one or both partners.

3. **Dislike for or by the other person's family.** Remember that this person is a product of that family. If your interests, values and philosophies do not match, how can you be good lifetime companions for each other? If the problem is that your family doesn't like the person you have chosen, maybe they can see things that you don't. At least listen to what they have to say. Don't let them decide for you. You are, after all, an independent, responsible person, but it is possible to be blinded by love or fear of loss.
4. **The relationship does not bring out the best in you.** Do you feel in a constant state of turmoil? Are you unhappy most of the time? Do you find that you do not like yourself and the way you behave anymore? Do you find yourself doing things you would prefer not to or being irritable over silly things? The important feeling in a relationship is not how the other person feels about you, but how you feel about yourself when you are with the person.
5. **The approach to marriage.** Is this marriage the result of an ultimatum? Have you known the person less than a year? Have you had several break-ups/make-ups? If you are saying, "I don't think it will work, but I'm going to give it a try. We can always get a divorce," watch out. Serious doubts indicate serious problems. Pay attention now.

Marriage is one of your options. However, you must remember that you can be happy and fulfilled without it if you choose. Nothing is more alone than being alone with someone. If it looks like the potential marriage is doomed from the beginning, get out. The world is populated with billions of men and this is not the only chance for marriage you are able to have. If marriage is your goal, find someone more suited to your needs.

Yes, ending a long-term (even a short-term, involved) relationship is painful. But no one dies from heartbreak. You will eventually be able to get past the pain and get on with your life. You will have learned more about your own needs and you will be better able to make a wiser choice for yourself in future relationships.

Chapter 9
THE DATING DILEMMA

Maybe marriage is not an immediate goal. Perhaps you are sitting there saying you'd be happy just to have more than one date with the same man. This is probably the most common complaint I hear from women today. "We met, he asked me out, we had a pleasant evening and I never heard from him again."

Many women interpret a man's lack of interest in a second date as rejection. At the very least, they are confused, especially if his final words were, "I'll call you." Why did he say he would call and then not do so? Who knows? It could be for any number of reasons, some of them probably the same ones women have for encouraging a man to call and then being less than receptive when he does. Perhaps one day we will begin to be honest with each other and say straight out, "I had a nice evening, but I don't think there is any reason to pursue this further. The chemistry just isn't there." Or whatever one might say to indicate that there is no further interest. Until then, both men and women need to realize that a date is only a one-time commitment, not an obligation for a lifetime. If we look at the dates we have as just that, we can all relax, be at our best and enjoy ourselves more completely. We can check each other out and decide if we want to see each other again without the pressure to make a commitment for a long-term relationship.

It is important, however, to look at some reasons why a second date doesn't happen. The number one reason has to be that there was no sense of connectedness — chemistry, if you will. You are both nice people but neither of you is what the other is looking for. This is a very valid reason. It doesn't make either of you a reject. It only means that there is no interest in pursuing a relationship with this person.

It always amazes me to see women feeling rejected because a man did not call for a second date within a week when their own reaction to the man was less than enthusiastic. You know, "He was okay and I had a pleasant evening. If he calls again, I'll go out with him but there wasn't any real chemistry there." Are you really interested in trying to form a romantic connection to someone like this or would you rather try someone else more suited to you?

The real problem arises if you were truly enthusiastic about the possible beginning of a relationship and he never calls again. In that case, try giving him a call. If his reaction is less than positive, if he doesn't appear glad to hear from you or is evasive, remember that attitude is everything. Instead of feeling like a reject, why not try some of the following responses? "He's terrific and that gives me hope. If there's one like him out there, there has to be more." Or, "It's his loss. I'm really a wonderful person and there will be someone else in my life soon." Or, "Maybe we just met at the wrong time."

Choose any reaction you like except one of berating yourself. It may not even have anything to do with you. I once went out with a man who literally overwhelmed me by being everything I thought I was looking for in a man. When he didn't call me, I called him to ask him to join me for a play to which I already had tickets. He was warm and friendly and explained to me that he had been dating a couple of other women when he met me. He said he had truly enjoyed my company but he didn't have the time or inclination to date several women at the same time and had settled on one of the others. He added that he was glad to have met me and wished me a happy future in a very complimentary way. I felt good. I even felt encouraged to keep looking for someone to have an ongoing relationship with because, as I stated earlier, if there's one out there, there must be more.

While the number one reason for no second date is the lack of a sense of connectedness, there are other reasons to consider. Some of them, unfortunately, have to do with the way a woman behaves or the kind of impression she makes. So if the no-second-date syndrome has been a problem for you, let's take a look at how you may have acted on the first date.

Did your date get your full and undivided attention? He deserved it. If you spent the whole evening or luncheon or coffee date wondering about the impression you were making, he probably didn't. If you didn't make eye contact during conversation, he probably didn't feel like he did. This was only a date, you were not interviewing for the CEO position at a major corporation so a few mistakes wouldn't have made that much difference. That means you needed to forget about the state of your make-up, hair and dress. You were supposed to take care of those things before you began the date.

Did you engage in conversation in a give-and-take manner? Or was the whole conversation a series of questions and answers? Did it ever get to a free-flowing exchange of information and ideas? None of us likes to force conversation. It is exhausting to do so and we won't volunteer for such heavy-duty work in the future if it can be avoided. Hence, no second date. Don't worry about saying something stupid. Everybody does at times, especially when tense. On the other hand, did you monopolize the conversation so that he had to work to get in a word or two? Free-flowing give-and-take is the rule here.

Did the second impression of you match the first? First impressions do count. Obviously you made a good one or you wouldn't have had a date to begin with. Even if that first contact was a phone call such as those we get through the personals or blind dates, you must have made a positive impression. If you were pretending to be something you are not, it may be difficult to carry off the second contact. Were you outgoing and friendly during the first encounter but quiet and reserved during the second? Did that quiet persona come across as aloof? Were you dressed appropriately for the occasion? If you were uncertain about dress, perhaps you should have asked somebody. If you were picked up at your home, was it ready to be seen? If you are neat and clean about yourself but live in a hovel, the first and second impressions do not match. Is it empty and temporary looking even though you have lived there for five years?

What was your dating focus? Were you negative all evening? If nothing went right, were you able to laugh at the situation or did you whine and complain? Did you spend the whole time talking about your ex? Did you lay out all of your past, current and future problems and concerns? Your date is neither a therapist nor a whipping post. He is a person you are supposed to have a pleasant time with.

Were you and your date complete opposites? If the answer to this one is yes, be glad you both recognized it so soon. Believe what people say. Just because you put a lot of energy and anticipation into this date, you don't have the right to try to change him into the person you wanted and thought you were getting.

Were you so desperate to put a man into your life that it showed? Needy women usually turn men off. Maybe you scared him off with your expectations. This is only a date, after all, and if you were making future noises and getting ready to plan a wedding, he will run fast and far. Even if you haven't been on a date in months, this is not the last man on earth and both of you need time to evaluate each other. If this man isn't the one, there will be others, especially if you relax and enjoy dating for what it is — a chance to have fun with another person.

Did you expect more than you had a right to? Again, this is only one date, not the rest of your life. If you thought you were going to be wined and dined and treated like a queen and all you got were a movie and coffee, so what? Especially if he paid the bill, you should have relaxed and had a good time. Maybe it takes him a while to decide to spend a lot of money on a woman. Did he ask you to pay half of the dinner check? Pay it graciously, then decide if this is how you would want to handle things in the future. If it's not, discuss it with him and make *your* decision about future dates with the information you gain.

Did you only talk about yourself all evening? Egocentricity is a major turn-off. You were supposed to be getting to know each other, not providing the complete and total history of you. No matter how exciting you think your life is or has been, nobody else will find it that fascinating on a first date.

What kind of physical activity occurred during the date? If you had sex, you probably shouldn't have. Why? Because you went from being strangers to being intimates without all the steps in between. This is usually a bad move. Not only is it a bad move, it's a dangerous one. How did you manage to ignore the possibility of disease? And sex on a first date leaves its own impression. No matter how desirable a man considers himself to be, he is going to have to wonder if you do this with everyone you go out with. No man wants a slut. Unless sex is all he really wants from you. If the two of you are willing to let that be the nature of your relationship, okay. It's your life. But I thought you were considering forming an ongoing relationship with all of the possibilities that can present. If you start with sex, that's probably where you will end up. If not after this date, maybe in a month or two, or perhaps in a year or two, but your chances of changing this relationship into a human one instead of a sexual one are limited.

Did you expect sex? Many men feel pressured to have sex. And many of them don't want to do so early in a relationship. If you are surprised to hear this, perhaps you need to take another look at men.

If you found yourself guilty of any of the preceding behaviors, don't berate yourself. Instead, make a concerted effort not to do it again. Learn from your mistakes. Consider all dates practice and use the past and future ones to improve your impression of you.

Please don't get defensive. The evaluation you just did is between you and yourself. Use it to create positives. Yes, I know you have a right to be the you that you are, but if it's getting in the way of your success in human relationships, it would be silly to hang on to unproductive behaviors and attitudes. Read through the following guidelines for dating and vow to follow them to the letter. I'll bet your track record for second, third, fourth and more dates will improve.

Guidelines for Dating

- Treat each date as what it is — a chance to enjoy yourself.
- Contribute to that enjoyment by being relaxed.
- Be pleasant no matter what happens. Even if you are disappointed, find something positive and focus on it.
- Smile, laugh, talk. Don't argue.
- Don't try to change the person.
- Have *human* relationships before *sexual* relationships.

Remember, nothing succeeds like success. Dating makes you feel better about yourself. It makes you feel more attractive, more open, more approachable. Haven't you noticed that meeting and dating new men seems to happen in spurts? When you are already dating someone, you seem to meet a lot of men. When you haven't had a date in a long time, you don't seem to meet anyone. Your attitude about yourself does make a difference.

One final point — there isn't any reason not to date a person you do not wish to marry as long as you both know this and are enjoying your time together. When it no longer brings you pleasure, that's the time to stop. Otherwise, use the dating relationship for practice and to give you an opportunity to present yourself as a confident and satisfied single person.

Chapter 10
ATTRACTIVENESS

If you have very few dates, I'll bet you occasionally question your appeal to the opposite sex. So before we deal with making connections with the opposite sex, the issue of attractiveness and your attitude about it has to be faced openly and honestly.

Beauty is in the eyes of the beholder. We each have our own standards which were created through years of evaluating the appearance of others, starting with our parents and other family members and moving to the peer group. Society also has a standard — unfortunately, a changing one. What's attractive today may be considered ugly or ridiculous tomorrow. So what's attractive and how do you become it?

First and foremost, you decide the kind of attractive you want to be. We each can and do develop a style which we believe reflects not only the image we have of ourself as a person but that we hope will be attractive to others. And that's where the problem appears. Often we project an image which satisfies us but turns off the very people we want to attract. For instance, observe the woman who aspires to get a job in a professional office or wants to attract a man who is a high-powered executive, yet she overpaints her face and dresses like a hooker. Or the woman who has two college degrees and dresses sloppily for a job interview or date.

I am not suggesting that you dress, style your hair or do your make-up in a way that is not you, but let's be real. There has to be a middle ground. Find your own sense of style and modify it to suit the situation. However, if you are definitely out of date or are so shabby that your clothes look like Salvation Army rejects, the reaction of most people is going to be "What a weirdo!" Or you will attract others like yourself. If that's what you want, terrific! Enjoy — it's your life.

If you are not enjoying the reactions of others and you don't like what you see when you look in the mirror, do some thinking and make some changes.

Do you make a "sleazy" impression when you dress? Are your clothes so tight they look sewn on? That's okay if you are the reincarnated Marilyn Monroe, but it's not okay for "real people." Are your breasts continually on display? Then no complaints when people speak to your chest instead of your face.

Do you look as if you spend every dollar you earn, and some that you haven't yet earned, on clothes? Whether you can afford to wear the latest fashions with impressive designer labels or not, you are making a statement. You may be telling the world that your values are a little skewed.

Do you look like you've been wearing the same clothes for last five years? Even if you have a very limited budget for clothing, you have no excuse for looking shabby. It just takes more planning and some shopping sense. The following guidelines may be helpful:

- Never buy anything without trying it on. This doesn't mean you have to do it in the store.

Unless you are buying a final sale item, you can usually take it home and return it if it doesn't work out. You have probably noticed some differences in home lighting and store lighting. Also, you don't always have the right accessories and undergarments on when you see that outfit you can't live without.

- Always try clothing on in front of a full length, preferably three-way, mirror. Check out the way the garment hangs. Look at the way it disguises or accentuates your figure plusses and flaws. If you don't have access to a three-way mirror, use a hand held one. What looks good from the front may make you look like an eggplant from the back.
- Even if it's in style, don't buy it if it looks terrible on you. Looking good and being comfortable are more important than being in style. Try to find another item or use current accessories with older styles that look good on you. There's more than one way to be in style.
- Do you have accessories such as shoes, jewelry and handbags to go with the items you are buying? If you don't, is it worth another $50.00 to $200.00 to include a particular dress or suit in your wardrobe?
- Can this garment be worn to more than one event? If all it is going to do is take up space in your closet after one wearing, keep looking until you find something more versatile.
- Always try on clothing with the appropriate undergarments. If a garment won't allow a bra, take yours off. If your breasts need the bra, find a

garment with built-in supports or buy press-on breast supports. If it is a dress or skirt you would wear with hose, don't try it on with sport socks.
- Undergarments must match. You don't wear navy blue pantyhose with a black skirt. You don't wear a white bra under a see-through dark garment.
- Don't buy a garment in a color that is bad for you just because it's the "in" color this year. If you are drained by the color, forget it or buy an accessory, such as a scarf, with the color in it.
- Consider the care and upkeep of the garments you buy. Dry cleaning can be expensive. Are you willing to pay the price? Dark clothing must be kept free of pet hairs, dandruff and lint. Many so-called permanent press garments require touch-up ironing. Will you be willing to do it?
- If you think a garment style will be a fad, buy it as cheaply as possible. When it goes out of style, you can toss it or wear it for cleaning the house without any real loss.
- Work your wardrobe purchases around a color scheme that will allow you to mix and match.

Following these suggestions will help you to use your clothing dollars wisely and to present yourself to the world as a person who both looks and feels attractive.

The way you dress tells the world about you. I believe that women fit into four categories of dressing: (1) blue jeans and up, (2) dressy/professional and down, (3) trendy, (4) ill-defined/pieced together. Each style of dressing makes a statement about the wearer and gets reactions from others.

Blue jeans and up. This woman is most comfortable in jeans and considers dressy casual to be dressed up. Seldom does she wear suits and dresses except to work, if her work requires it. Heels and hose are not her most comfortable mode and dressing for an evening at the theater or for dinner in an expensive restaurant is almost a chore. She gives the impression that she is much more comfortable going to less dressy places. And that's what she gets — invitations to less dressy places.

Dressy/professional and down. This woman dresses in a more formal style and enjoys it. She sees jeans as around-the-house wear, definitely not public or date wear. Her idea of casual is slacks and a nice blouse. Appropriate dress is important to her and she is making a statement about herself that says she prefers dinner and the theater to a movie and McDonald's. It doesn't mean she isn't open to other entertainments, just that she has definite preferences.

Trendy. The trendy woman is always clothed in the latest fashion trends. She believes her statement to the world is that she is in touch with style. That doesn't necessarily mean that the clothes look good on her. But they are the "right" color, length and shoulder width.

Unfortunately the statement she is making is easily misinterpreted and instead of coming across as "in," she comes across as insecure. If you are under college graduation age, this is okay because you are still defining yourself and may need this type of prop. If you are past the age of twenty-four, your wardrobe probably needs to contain a few more pieces of classic clothing and items with enough versatility to be worn next year.

Ill-defined/pieced together. The wardrobe of this woman looks exactly like what it is — a collection of items bought here and there. It doesn't quite create a cohesive whole. Sometimes it works, sometimes it doesn't. Because there has been little thought to a coordinated wardrobe that allows clothing to be combined into complete outfits, she frequently finds herself scrounging around for something to wear, looking frumpy or being dressed inappropriately. While she may have some lovely clothing, her appearance in general does not make a positive statement about the kind of woman she is. Her wardrobe may be saying that she has not yet defined herself and that she is still in the process of determining the kind of woman she wants to be.

The best wardrobe is one that suits your body type, your budget and your life style. It is an external manifestation of the inner you. If you are not attracting the kind of people you want in your life, take a look at the image you are presenting. If you want to be successful in situations with others, particularly members of the opposite sex, you have to dress for the part or at least give the impression that you are prepared to do so.

While we are talking about attractiveness, let's take a close look at that body you live in. Do you like it? If you do, stop reading here and go on to the next chapter. If your answer is no, stay with this one.

What is the shape of the shape you are in? Too big? Too small? Just right? For whom? Of course you have the right to be the size you choose, but if that size is getting in the way of your success in the relationships you want, maybe you should do something about it. I don't necessarily mean your relationships with others, although that may be one consideration. I mean your relationship to you. Are you comfortable in your own body? Do you condemn yourself every day for not losing weight? If you hate yourself for the shape or size of your body, either learn to like it or change it. There are too many fun and exciting things to use your time and energy on for you to waste them in self-hatred over your body.

Relationships with others may be a different consideration altogether. How many times have you heard women, including yourself, complain about how men only want slim, gorgeous women? No matter how fat, ugly and unattractive a man may appear to you, he still seems to demand that you be perfect. And instead of reacting with "What a jerk!" women tend to get defensive and ask "What about the beauty inside?" Yes, we are all beautiful on the inside, but if the outside is truly unattractive, no one is going to take the time or effort to look inside.

Yes, it is unfair, but let's not be hypocritical. I hear truly fat women reject men on externals like baldness, pot bellies and height. All of us have a mental image of the person we want and we hold fast to it through years of pain and loneliness. In this respect, men and women are very much alike. You can continue to complain, but let's face it, there are some things that fair or not, you may have to work on. If the people you want in your life are looking for what you are not, you will either have to change your goals or change some externals.

Let's look at fat. There are some men who like big women. Spend some time people watching in an area where there are a lot of couples. You will see a parade of chubbies with skinny guys who can't keep their hands off the ample layers of feminine flesh. However, if you are at all concerned about the health risks associated with being overweight, it may be time for you to develop a healthier, slimmer body. Do it for yourself, not to please a man. No, it isn't easy, but it is possible. There are hundreds of organizations, books, businesses and clinics ready and willing to help you for a price. But the formula is really simple and costs nothing. Reduce food intake, increase exercise.

Can it really be that simple? *Yes!* There is, however, a caution based upon the reality of millions of people who go up and down the poundage scale. The body is a homeostatic entity. That means it aims toward stability. Your body is comfortable with what it is used to. To keep weight off, you must create and maintain a new stability for your body. From everything I've read and heard about this theory, that takes three years.

If you have weighed 200 pounds for years, it will be harder for you to keep ten pounds off than someone who loses the ten pounds she gained during the holidays. Your body is comfortable with 200 pounds so it's going to take a concerted and ongoing effort to get your body to work with you. Once you get it off and keep it off for three years, it will be easy to stay slim.

Now, what about cost? People say, "I can't afford all those diet foods." You don't need to buy special foods. Regular foods, wisely selected, will do. A head of lettuce, even out of season for your area of the country, is around $1.29. A half-gallon of ice cream costs two or three times that much. Cookies are approximately $1.50 per pound. Apples are seldom more than $1.29 a pound.

And how much red meat do you really need to eat? Chicken costs a lot less than beef, is better for you and has fewer calories.

If you have never had a good course in nutrition, or have forgotten what you were taught, let me give you a quick lesson here.

Foods fit into six categories. You need a number of servings from each, every day, to have a well-balanced and healthful diet. Use the following as your guide.

Vegetables — 2-4 servings per day. One should be rich in Vitamin A. You get Vitamin A from dark green and deep yellow vegetables.

Fruits — 3-5 servings per day. One serving should be high in Vitamin C. You get Vitamin C from citrus fruits.

The vegetables and fruits in your diet provide you with the vitamins and minerals you need to keep your body functioning properly. You also get fiber to aid in good digestion. As an added plus, Vitamin A is essential for skin health, so if you are getting your greens and yellows every day, your skin will have a glow of health.

Meat, Fish, Eggs & Poultry — 2 servings daily. This group is your major source of complete protein which is needed to keep your body alive and well. This is a food group where you get lots of choice for calorie variation. You can eat turkey for low calories, fish for low calories or you can choose lots of beef for high calories. Eggs are high in cholesterol but they are also an excellent source of protein. You don't, however, need to have two every morning. This group also includes lentils, nuts and peanut butter.

Dairy Products — 2 servings daily. Calcium is the major reason for making sure you get these two servings each day. However, milk and cheese also provide good quality protein. Again, you can vary the calorie content. White cheeses tend to be lower in calories than yellow cheeses. Skim milk and yogurt have less calories than whole milk.

Breads, Cereals, Pasta, and Whole Grain Products — 6-11 servings daily. Your level of activity determines whether you need six or eleven. Most women, even if they exercise vigorously on a daily basis, do not need eleven. Whenever possible, make them whole grain. DO NOT SKIP YOUR BREAD SERVINGS! If you get crabby and listless and don't lose weight as fast as you would like to, it's probably because you decided to cut out the bread products. The bread servings are high in carbohydrates — that's where you get energy. The bread servings are high in the B-vitamins which are necessary for nervous health and good digestion. Not only do whole grain products provide fiber, they also give you B-6 which you need to prevent nausea and other digestive problems. Carbohydrate foods usually have B-12 which is a natural tranquilizer. And of great importance, you need the B-vitamins to break down fat cells so that you can get rid of them.

Fats, Oils and Sweets — Use sparingly. This means that you need some fat in your diet but not a lot. If more than 30% of your calories come from fat, you are gaining weight. The fat you eat is the fat you wear. Use caution, when using reduced fat, low fat, or non-fat products since it's easy to convince yourself that it's okay to eat more than usual. It's not.

What about desserts and sweet things like candy? Have them — but in small amounts. I highly recommend a spoonful of ice cream and I mean just that. Don't get a dish, get a soup spoon, fill it full and eat. You don't need a lot to satisfy yourself. Same thing with other sweets and goodies that you just can't resist. Take a taste. You don't have to eat the whole thing.

Pick the low calorie items from each food group. Spread them throughout the day and enjoy. Plan in some snacks. Popcorn is a good one since it's low in calories and is quite filling. Just don't drown it in butter.

Next, exercise. That's the way to get the weight off in the places you want it off. Do you need to join a gym or buy special equipment? Not unless you want to. You can go to the library and find a book that will allow you to plan your own exercise program. If you don't want to do that, walk a couple of miles each day. Use it as your time to smell the roses or azaleas or lilacs or whatever is blooming in your neighborhood. Appreciate the beauty of the sky, the feeling of the breeze on your skin, the sounds and smells of your world. You will feel great. Exercise does more to perk you up than to tire you out. I guarantee that you will feel better after a thirty-minute walk than you will after a thirty-minute nap.

There is one more topic which must be addressed as part of the attractiveness of the physical image each of us presents to the world. That topic is posture. The way you stand, walk and sit makes a significant difference in the way you look. Standing straight with your head held high can make you look ten pounds thinner and make your clothes fit and look better on you. Women who slump look dumpy. Walking tall, regardless of your height, improves your appearance.

Women who stand tall tend to develop a more energetic and attractive stride as they walk. They look more coordinated. Women who sit tall look confident. Those who sink into themselves when sitting look lifeless. They appear to be both uninterested and uninteresting.

If you have never learned to stand up straight and to carry yourself with pride and dignity (not the same as stiffness — good movement has a flow), now is the time to do it. Practice walking with a book balanced on your head. Sounds stupid, but it works to improve posture. Do it every day until walking straight feels natural. Whenever you think of it, straighten yourself up whether you are standing, sitting or walking. Pretend there is a string running through the middle of your body and visualize yourself pulling up the slack. Suck in your belly. If you don't believe this makes a difference, do it in front of a full length mirror. What you see will convince you. Posture does make a difference.

If you wear shoes with heels or platforms most of the time, practice walking in a flowing way. And watch the height of the heels — if you end up walking like a robot, they are too high for you. Nothing destroys the attractive look of a well-put-together woman faster than a jerking stride caused by shoes in which she can't walk with a graceful flow.

I hope that this chapter has given you information that will help you to become the kind of attractive you want to be. The choice is yours to make. Evaluate the options in light of the goals you want to achieve. Then advance confidently in that direction.

Chapter 11
UNATTRACTIVENESS

Okay, you have taken care of your physical attractiveness and are presenting yourself as the best you can be, but you still aren't experiencing the kind of success you want in relationships with others, especially opposite sex others. Maybe it's not your physical appeal, but your personality appeal that is creating problems. Physical appeal may draw the attention of others to you, personality appeal is what will keep it there. Maybe you are driving people away without realizing it because you are engaging in one or more of the behaviors this chapter details.

You do have the right to be and do whatever you choose, but it is important to evaluate those choices if they are getting in the way of your success in human relationships. Some behaviors are clearly obnoxious. They turn others off. The following discussion presents an even "dirty dozen" of such behaviors.

1. **Egocentricity.** If all you can talk about is yourself and the activities you engage in, people are going to tire of you very quickly. You may find yourself and your life fascinating, but few others will enjoy spending hours in conversation about you and you alone. The only cure for this is to make a conscious effort to talk about other people and other things. The range of topics available to you is unlimited.

2. **Talking too much/talking too little.** Let's start with talking too much. This can be related to egocentricity, but its cause frequently lies elsewhere. It is a habit which may have started in childhood. Children who do this are called "chatterbox children" and parents are encouraged to help such children learn that there are times to talk and times to listen. Talking too much gets in the way of a child's social relationships. It also gets in the way of an adult's social relationships.

Sometimes its cause is nervousness. The gaps in conversation create tension so you rush to fill them with words. Even if you are uncomfortable with silent periods, you don't need to fill every moment with verbiage. Try using the periods of silence to appreciate where you are and who you are with. Practice doing this. Over time, you will learn that silence can be golden if you let it be. In fact, one sign of a truly comfortable relationship with another person is allowing each other to be alone with thoughts while you are together. A quiet touch, a wink or an occasional smile can let the other person know that you are still aware of and appreciative of his or her company.

The cure for talking too much is to practice being quiet. Focus on listening to others instead of thinking about the next thing you are going to say.

Talking too little often puts pressure on the other person to draw you out. It becomes a question-and-answer session and is a very exhausting process for the questioner. The cause of talking too little may also go back to childhood if a person was raised in a home where the conversation of children was not listened to or encouraged. It may also be caused by nervousness or fear of not being interesting enough for others to pay attention to. Whatever the cause, one must practice to change this habit.

3. **Talking too fast/talking too slow.** These problems may also have their roots in childhood. Talking too fast is more common in people who come from large families where competition for talk time is great. Talking too slowly can be caused by parents who constantly correct children's speech and pronunciation. Both may have roots in situations where people are afraid of being interrupted or ignored.

   Regardless of cause, it is difficult to listen to a fast talker or a slow talker. Much of what the fast talker says doesn't register with the listener. Much of what the slow talker says is missed because the listener is busy mentally finishing sentences instead of paying attention to what is being said. Both practices get in the way of pleasant conversation with others. The only cure for either is to make a concerted effort to change the rate at which words leave your mouth.

4. **Negativity.** If talking with you is a bummer because you seldom have anything positive to say, or if you are continually critical of the ideas and activities of others, you will soon be left out of social situations altogether. Review your remarks in conversations and evaluate the

amount of time you spend focused on the negative. If it is frequent, rather than rare or occasional, make a concentrated effort to develop a more positive view of life. Practice saying positive things and looking for the pleasant side of situations. If you can't find anything good or pleasant in a situation, look for the lessons to be learned. If you can't find those either, shut up and listen.

5. **"Rightness" behaviors.** These behaviors include argumentativeness and pettiness along with controlling behaviors like power plays and manipulation. If you have to be in charge or have your own way most of the time, if you complain about little things or argue over issues and details, people are going to avoid being in your presence. Life is not a contest. However, you can make yourself into a loser in the game of life by turning others off to a possible relationship with you. If being right holds great importance for you, if you have a vested interest in proving that you are right, and therefore others are wrong, you may find yourself becoming a very lonely person.

If you know you are right, why do you have to have others agree with you? Allowing others the freedom to have their own opinions and ideas is important to the give and take of human relationships. The only power you need in relationships is power over you. You can't change other people anyway, so why would you want to use your energy trying to do so? Manipulating others does not show respect for them as human beings and indicates a feeling of powerlessness in yourself. At some point in your life, you are going to have to realize that manipulation of others indicates a lack of trust in other people's interest in you and your way of living. The need to control also indicates a lack of security on your part. Controlling behaviors turn people off and create anger and unpleasantness within relationships. If you find yourself engaging in such behaviors frequently, perhaps some therapy is needed to rid you of the causes such as unexpressed anger, insecurity and feelings of worthlessness.

6. **Little girl behaviors.** A real man wants a real woman. So do other grown-up women. A real woman is one who can take care of herself and has confidence in her own abilities, one who is not prone to silliness. There is a major difference between being child-like and being childish. A person who is child-like is one who has not forgotten the pleasure little things can bring, one who can experience the world with wonder and joy, one who can laugh freely and easily. A childish person is one who pouts, gets angry or cries when she doesn't get her way, one who expects to be the center of attention. She does not appear to have competence in any area of living. She needs to be entertained and taken care of. She can't accept constructive criticism and takes no responsibility for her behaviors and actions. It's always someone else's fault if things go wrong. She shows little impulse control and says and does whatever comes to mind without thinking

about consequences. She calls this spontaneity. Usually it's just rude and irresponsible. There is only one cure for little girl behaviors. Grow up! Watch the behaviors of others who appear mature and sophisticated. Emulate it.

7. **Rude behaviors.** We all know what these are. We recognize them easily when they are done to us but seem to view them differently when we are the doers. They include being insulting to others, saying rude things, cutting ahead in line, pushing and shoving and so forth. Sometimes it's humor at the expense of others, name calling, interrupting others, not excusing one's self when walking away from another in conversation. In its milder forms, it's a simple lack of courtesy like not saying please, thank you, excuse me or I'm sorry when the situation calls for it. There is no excuse for any of the above. Not even in response to the rudeness of others. The cure — just don't do them. Practice courteous behaviors at all times.

8. **Insecurity, neediness and jealousy.** People who continually need reassurance of their attractiveness, worth or role in a relationship are exhibiting signs of insecurity. Security comes from within and no amount of reinforcement can create what isn't there to begin with. There is a gigantic difference between liking compliments and needing them. We all need a pat on the back occasionally and the pats are nice to get even when we don't feel the need for them, but those who need constant ego stroking exhaust us.

Jealousy is frequently an insecurity problem. Others have something we don't, so we feel that we can't measure up. Or we think that others are so special that they may be able to take what we have away from us. A jealous woman often shows her jealousy by making disparaging comments about others or by demanding reinforcement of her worth and role in a person's life. Having to constantly reassure others of our love for them gets old very quickly and we begin to withdraw from contact. It just takes too much energy to stick around.

The only way to deal with these feelings and behaviors is to take a good look at your own positives and stroke yourself. Become a more secure person and you will find you don't need to depend on others for validation of your worth.

9. **Dishonesty and insincerity.** These two sides of the same coin create all sorts of problems in human relationships. When people discover that we have been dishonest with them, they feel betrayed and find it difficult to trust the things we say and do. Insincerity is a mild form of dishonesty that can be equally hurtful because it is usually used in a manipulative way. Neither creates warm, open, free-flowing human relationships. The only way to fix this one is to tell the truth.

10. **Neurotic behaviors.** This set of behaviors includes continual worrying and constant messes in one's life. If your life is in a constant state of turmoil,

the only way others can relate to you is to get sucked into your problems or to be on call to hear you tell of the latest crises or worry in your life. It just takes too much energy to be involved with you.

Chances are that the people you do attract have as much difficulty handling day-to-day living as you do and have few reasonable solutions to offer. Many of the solutions you offer to each other are more self-defeating than the ones you have already tried. This continual focus on problems leaves little time and energy for the more positive, more fun side of life. If life is one hassle after another, my suggestion is that you seek out a competent therapist and work to free yourself of this behavior pattern.

11. **Addictive behaviors.** People who drink too much, smoke, do drugs or eat compulsively are displaying addictive behaviors. All of these behaviors are turn-offs and each may require professional help to get you past the problem. The one you may be able to control by yourself is smoking. If you choose not to quit smoking, you will have to accept the fact that many people will not date smokers. Some people will not allow smoking in their homes or cars. If you continue to smoke, recognize the fact that you may be eliminating a significant portion of the population from the group of people you could possibly relate to. This is a choice you get to make, but you have no cause to complain about the consequences of your choice.

12. **Smells.** In our society, it is expected that people will bathe regularly, wash their hair when it needs it, use deodorant and wear clean clothes. If you stink, you turn people off. However, body odors are not the only offensive smells. Some of the perfumes and colognes on the market are equally offensive. Wearing too much of any scent can be overpowering.

I once, and may I emphasize the once, went out with a man who wore a scent that smelled like industrial strength janitor-in-a-drum. I avoid all contact with a woman I know because she wears a perfume that gives me a headache. Yes, I did tactfully explain the problem to her. She chose to continue wearing the perfume; I chose to avoid her.

Bad breath is a definite turn-off. If you have a halitosis problem, see a physician or dental professional. Of course, you will floss and brush your teeth and tongue regularly.

That's the dirty dozen. You can probably add more but the major ones have been covered. Whether we accept it as fair or not, each of us must "sell" ourselves and we can't do an effective job of selling if we are presenting defective or flawed merchandise. Again, you have the right to be and do whatever you choose, but it is important to evaluate those choices if they are getting in the way of your success in human relationships.

Chapter 12
THE PLACE WHERE YOU LIVE

The impression you make through the environment you create is the third element to be considered in a discussion on attractiveness. The first two, physical appeal and personality appeal, interact synergistically when added to the third. The sum of the parts exceeds the total. If all three parts match, they give others a balanced and positive impression. If they don't, the impression is unbalanced, confusing and negative. A woman may think that discrepancy in one of the areas shows her to be multi-faceted. It doesn't. It just leaves a bad impression, a disappointing one, or one in which people just don't know what to think of her. So they stop thinking of her. One element out of sync may cause a woman to be left out of the social scene, particularly the dating scene. If she is gorgeous, but has the personality of a doorknob, she is not appealing. If she is gorgeous, with a pleasant personality, but lives like a slob, she is successful only until someone comes to her home.

The place where you live says a lot about you as a person. We are not talking about addresses here, although that could be a consideration. We are talking about decoration and comfort. We are not talking about cost, we're talking about creating a pleasant, warm and welcoming environment.

You are entitled to furnish and decorate your home any way you like because the most important person to consider when you establish your home environment is, of course, you. But certain general considerations are important.

Is your environment clean? I have been in homes that feel dirty. I don't even want to sit down because I know that I will feel the need to bathe and have my clothes cleaned when I leave.

It's not necessary to clean every day or even every week, but floors shouldn't be sticky and heavy dust and cobwebs should not be in evidence. Messy and dirty are not the same thing. In a messy environment, a basic cleanliness is obvious. If a little picking up will create a clean looking environment, that's messy. If picking up still doesn't create the impression of cleanliness, that's dirty.

Each of us, men included, has our own standard of cleanliness. Some people can handle more mess than others, but some things are unacceptable to all. Things like a greasy stove, dried food on counters, a mildew-covered bathroom, dirty toilet bowls, filthy floors, badly stained carpets and windows that can't be seen through are real turn-offs for almost everyone.

If the whole idea of cleaning your environment overwhelms you, hire someone. Or find a system that will accomplish it with a minimum of effort on your part. I would recommend taking a couple of days to do a thorough cleaning. Then make a concerted effort to keep it that way.

My home always looks clean, but I spend little time cleaning. Once a year, I do a thorough cleaning that includes cleaning closets and cupboards. The rest of the year, I clean once a month. I dust, vacuum and clean the bathroom. That's all it takes because I pick up and put things away every day before I go to bed. The kitchen is cleaned up with a few wipes each time I use it. The bathroom is done the same way.

If you live alone, there is no excuse for mess or dirt. If you have a roommate or children, there is still no excuse. Everyone does a share. Remember, if a child can walk, he can pick up after himself.

Your home must smell clean, too. The fact that you have a pet should not be obvious when someone enters your home. If you have a cat, that means cleaning the litter every day. If you have a dog, it must be completely house broken. If you have an aquarium, the water must be clean and clear. If you have a bird, it must be kept in a cage so that it doesn't leave droppings everywhere. Piles of laundry and overflowing waste baskets, especially in the kitchen, smell. College students can get away with that, adult women can't.

Again, you are selling an impression of yourself to others. Would you shop in a dirty, messy or smelly store? A personal environment that is unclean and smells says you don't care about yourself and others. The impression your home makes counts.

Men, in particular, will note the environment you create. Even if a man is messy, he will evaluate your interest in and ability to create a home whether he wants to marry you or not. Fair? Maybe not, but before you start raging about the way single men live, I think you should take a closer look. Most of the single men I know live in clean, well-decorated homes, condos or apartments.

Secondly, what does the decor say about you? The furniture and furnishings in your home should present a coordinated whole that says something positive about the kind of person you are. That doesn't mean it has to look like something straight out of *Town and Country* or *Metropolitan Home*, but it should be at least a step above garage sale potpourri. You can mix different styles and periods of furniture, but the mixture should create a unified whole that allows comfort for you and others. Your home must look like someone enjoys living in it and it must have a sense of completeness about it. It shouldn't look temporary. Even if you plan to live somewhere less than six months, your personal environment should still look organized and comfortable.

You can use other people's give-aways and garage sale purchases but they should be tasteful and clean and fit together. Antiques are fine, but not for sitting. Except for rocking chairs and some dining room chairs, most antique seating pieces are not comfortable.

As a minimum, you must have a sofa, a table with chairs and something to sleep on. Anyone who comes to your home must have a place to sit down comfortably whether you are eating, talking or whatever.

Frequently, it's not the furniture, but the furnishings that make the difference between a good impression and a negative one. Furnishings include items such as throw pillows, knick-knacks, artworks, plants, lamps and so forth. If you are an adult, you must show it in your decorating choices. Cutesy wallpaper (you know, naked people behind towels on bathroom walls) and *Mickey Mouse* toaster covers do not belong in an adult woman's home. Her decor should reflect the fact that she is a grown-up. Stuffed animals are not appropriate. They say she is still an insecure little girl who isn't ready to relate to an adult man in an ongoing relationship. Antique toys like a hobby horse, doll house or wicker carriage may be used if they fit the rest of the decor. If you have a collection of tops or dolls, put them in a cabinet or on a set of shelves so that it's obvious they are a collection, not play things.

While the furniture and furnishings set the major tone, other factors contribute to the ambience. Color is a significant contributor to the comfort of the environment you create. Not enough color is boring. Colors that are too bright or garish are overstimulating and unsettling.

Temperature plays a role. It shouldn't be too hot or too cold. If you have a fire in the fireplace, remember to turn down the central heating thermostat. If you are having a group of people over, with or without a fireplace, it will heat up quickly. If you don't have air conditioning, oven-prepared meals for company are not appropriate in the heat of summer.

I am acutely aware of the effect of temperature because I have a friend who likes it cold. Whenever I visit her in the winter, I have to take an extra sweater or wear my coat during the entire visit. Needless to say, I don't feel welcome in her home for anything more than a short visit.

Sounds are also an important part of the environment you create. You don't need an elaborate or expensive stereo system, complete with CD player, but background music can be soothing and create an atmosphere of warmth. Not only can you use it for your own relaxation and pleasure, but it can provide entertainment for you and your guests.

Is your home ready for company? This question goes beyond clean and comfortably furnished and addresses the items it contains behind closed doors. Do you have equipment for cooking and eating? You don't have to have matching pots and pans, but your pots should have handles and should not have burned-on food or grease stains. You don't need fine china and sterling silver, but you should have a matched set of dishes and a complete set of stainless flatware. Earthenware is inexpensive. You can probably get place settings for eight in white for $50.00 or less on sale. White allows you to set a table for both elegant and casual meals. You can get quality stainless flatware on sale for about $50.00. Matching glasses, including wine glasses, can be gotten for about $50.00. This $150.00 may be your best spent money for several years to come.

Your refrigerator and cupboards don't have to be full of food at all times, but you should be able to put together some kind of meal on short notice. You don't have to be a gourmet cook, but you should show some competence with simple meals without having to run to the store. That means having some ingredients on hand. I suggest that you prepare some home cooked foods for the freezer, things like burgundy beef or chili or anything that will last for a while in the frozen state. Some frozen vegetables and rolls will help you to put together an impressive meal quickly.

You should have a supply of coffee grounds (not instant coffee), tea and wine (both red and white) available at all times. Cold pop, beer and fruit juices are also useful beverages to have available. Why? Because you should always be ready to have guests. A guest is anyone who doesn't live in your home. Regardless of how long you have known them, visitors deserve a warm welcome. Snack foods like cheese and crackers keep for a long time and are quick and acceptable refreshments. Vegetables with dip (ranch dressing can be used) and fresh fruits are also useful as snacks for guests and, I hope they are a normal part of your diet as well.

If you occasionally have overnight guests, male or female, you should be prepared. That means you have a few new toothbrushes and disposable razors in your home. You also need to have at least two sets of towels that are not frayed or stained.

I consider candles an essential item, both as part of the decor and as part of entertaining others. Shop for them during after-Christmas sales. Fabric stores, craft shops and card shops frequently put them on sale after the holidays. Buy as many boxes as you can afford, especially white ones, and use them throughout the year.

That takes care of the inside. What about the outside? If you own your own home, the yard needs regular care that includes mowing and watering. In the winter, walks and porches must be cleared of snow and ice. If you can't do it, hire someone. Just make sure it gets done.

If you don't believe the environment you create is important in the impression you make, think about your reaction the first time you entered the home of each of your friends. Did you ever change your opinion of anyone, male or female, based on a visit to his or her living space? Do you find yourself very comfortable in some homes and very uncomfortable in others?

Face it. Your home is a reflection of you. It tells people about your values and interests. If it's not saying anything positive about you right now, change it. Do something that will bring it into alignment with the other positive parts of you.

Chapter 13
ATTRACTING MEN

Since Adam and Eve, people have been trying to figure out how to attract members of the opposite sex. Adam and Eve had it relatively easy. They were the only man and woman on earth. You, however, have literally millions to choose from which means you have to set some standards for yourself. You even have the freedom to make comments like "I wouldn't marry him if he were the last man on earth." Since you know he's not, you can afford to be choosy.

"Not so," you say. "I can't seem to find anyone who fits." Or, "The men I want don't seem to want me, but the men I don't want won't go away." What a dilemma! You want to choose someone who chooses you back, right?

If you see yourself as the "chooser," you are way ahead of the majority of single women, most of whom are waiting to be chosen by the right man (whatever that is). In addition to being the chooser, you have to figure out what you are looking for. Not what you think you'll get, but what you truly must have to form a long-lasting and satisfying relationship. Even those of us who do not have marriage as an immediate goal want loving relationships with members of the opposite sex to continue over time.

Identifying what you really want and need will be

addressed later in this chapter. We need to focus first on what the sexes find attractive in each other. People have been trying to unravel this particular mystery for centuries. Since no one has arrived at the definitive answer yet, I'll share my theory. It's as good as any other that I've heard and makes sense to me.

There are basically four things that women find appealing about men — power, money, physical appearance and being a nice guy. Men can balance out a lack in one area by combining elements of the others. A good example of this is the older man who dates, and then, marries a woman who is twenty or more years younger than himself. What he lacks in physical appearance, he is able to make up for in power and money.

Some elements have more initial attraction value than others. A man who is tall, handsome and nicely built doesn't need to have power or money to attract women. He doesn't even have to be a nice guy.

Unfortunately for men, being a nice guy isn't enough. Niceness has to be combined with one or more of the other elements to make the man desirable to women.

Whether you agree or not, whether it's fair or not — and we all know it isn't — men have power just because they are men. In fact, when women don't see themselves as choosers, men are given even more power. Men get additional power through social position, intelligence and education.

Each woman ranks the four elements of appeal according to her own standards of desirability. Some women only want to date men with money. Some women only want to date powerful men or men who have power jobs. Some women only date handsome men who fit the ideal of their generation. Seldom does a woman date a man on his nice guy image alone.

We all deal in a system of trade-offs. If we choose to have or get one thing, we usually have to give up having or getting something else. We can't have it all regardless of what some self-help books tell us. A man can trade on his looks, his position of power or his money, but he doesn't often get to trade on being a nice guy alone.

"Oh, no! That's not true," you say. Well, when was the last time you dated a nice unemployed man? He may have been a perfect gentleman, filled with honesty and integrity, who wanted the same things as you do, but that wasn't enough. In fact, many women will allow a man to treat them badly as long as he continues to provide an income or is good looking enough to draw attention from others.

Women, on the other hand, are at what could be considered a disadvantage. There are only two elements they can trade on to attract men. One is physical appearance. The other is nurturance (the female side of the nice guy coin). A woman who has power and money may have a certain appeal to men, but she can't balance out a lack of physical appeal with them. Women are expected to be nurturant, to provide support and comfort to a man. A woman is expected to create a home even if she works. After all, isn't that what Mom did or was supposed to do? If she didn't, society said there was something wrong with Mom, not that it shouldn't have been expected of her.

To make matters worse, men have some unique ideas about what makes a woman appealing. Dumb stuff

— like hair color and breasts. I have never known a woman who chooses men by their hair color. Nor do I know any "leg women" or "shoulder women" but I frequently hear men describe themselves as "breast men" or "leg men."

So a woman is left with the task of trying to figure out what she can do to make herself physically appealing to men. That's why we have racks full of "women's" magazines, each one featuring monthly articles on how to be attractive, how to find a man and how to keep him interested once you get him. There are very few major men's magazines that even come close to dealing with such issues. Most self-help books, including this one, are written primarily for women.

In the end, there is no sure way to be appealing to men because each man has his own ideas about the subject. It depends on the man. A woman has to fit a man's image of the woman he is looking for. Thus, it becomes trophyism. Each man has an idea of the woman he is looking for and when he finds her, he will do whatever is necessary to capture her heart. That's why dating is sometimes referred to as "the chase."

Let me give you a couple of examples of this from men I have known. I used to socialize with, and occasionally date, a man who very candidly told me that I was "almost perfect for him, but not quite." He couldn't define what he found "not quite perfect" about me, but in some way, I didn't match the image he had of his perfect woman.

A man I dated many years ago proposed to me. I asked him why he wanted to marry me since all we seemed to do was argue and disagree. Without hesitation, he replied that I "fit the image of the woman he should have for a wife." Now that's trophyism in its ultimate form.

Each woman also has an image of the man she should have, but women, in general, are more willing to compromise. They make trade-offs more easily.

"Wait," you are saying. "What about things like intelligence, education, high paying/high power employment for women?" To be encouraged — yes. Promoted — no. Many men are still threatened by these things if a woman has more or better than they do. In our society, men still marry down the socio-economic scale, women still marry up. Ironically, this fact has created a problem for men under the age of 34 because there are now more single men than single women in each age group below 34. Women have married men one or more years older (more appealing because of better jobs, more money, more power) leaving men of their own age in the lurch.

The factors of intelligence, education, high paying/high power employment rank for women about as high as being a nice guy does for men. They are only valuable when combined with attractiveness or nurturance. They may, in fact, be detrimental to a relationship, if she surpasses him. A man I was involved with decided there was no potential for a marriage in our relationship because I was college educated and he was not. Inspite of the satisfactions our relationship appeared to provide in many areas, including hours of pleasant conversation, he said that he felt stupid when he was with me. He said that he felt that way because my vocabulary was larger than his. The exact words he used were that he "frequently didn't know what the hell I was talking about".

Is all of the above fair? No. Is it beginning to change? Yes. Both men and women are beginning to reevaluate, but right now, it is reality. So what's a woman to do? Well, you can complain about it, but you'll probably find yourself spending a lot of time alone if you do. Or you can work to change the way things are.

Chances of changing men over 50 are slim to none. Men under that age are changing and women must support their efforts. In addition to that, we must raise our sons differently. We must help them to develop their nurturing and homemaking skills and to value women for their competencies not just their physical appeal.

We must teach our daughters to value themselves for characteristics besides beauty. We must help them to set and achieve goals that will allow them to use their intelligence and to follow their interests. We must be role models for them. Otherwise, a hundred years from now men and women will still be appraised by the standards we use today, standards which say a woman is how she looks, a man is what he does.

We must also claim some power for ourselves. One of the best ways to do this is to give ourselves permission to choose in male-female relationships. We do not have to be at the mercy of men. We can function without them if we choose. We prefer not to because men can enhance our lives through the relationships we have with them. Since we *choose* to have them in our lives, we should also *choose* which of the many available we want. We can do this only if we stop knocking ourselves out trying to find the perfect look to make ourselves appealing to them. We can develop an image for ourselves which is, first and foremost, satisfying to each of us as an individual. When each of us chooses the kind of attractive she wants to be, we will be free of the constraints that trying to satisfy the male image of what we should be imposes upon us.

This is going to take time and effort and it won't happen overnight, but it will happen. Does all of this contradict the information and suggestions in Chapter 10? No. Even in the discussions on attractiveness, you were encouraged to satisfy your idea of appealing while presenting an image that reflects the lifestyle that you have chosen for yourself. If a man is attracted to the image you create, especially if that image truly reflects you and your choice of lifestyle, there's a good chance that he will be the type of man you want to attract.

What does all of this mean in terms of the old myth about opposites attracting? Not much. Primarily because the myth of opposites attracting is a misunderstood one. The myth originally meant that complements attract — we choose someone who provides something we are missing. A calm, quiet person chooses an outgoing, vibrant, witty person. A weak person chooses strength in a mate. And so on and so on. Despite such choices, the myth remains a myth because we cannot depend upon someone else to complete us, to provide what we don't have. That makes us dependent, not interdependent. It creates relationships of need, not relationships of choice.

No one can be you. Therefore, you must become a complete person all by yourself. Why? Because the other way of doing it doesn't work. People have been trying to make it work for generations and it just doesn't. In fact, over time, the other person gets tired of having to make up for your lacks. Resentment develops. It also doesn't work because it limits growth. If you choose someone who will do "it" for you, you never learn to do "it" for yourself. And if you do learn to do it for yourself, you no longer need the other person and the relationship no longer has a purpose. Thus, the sayings, "we outgrew each other" or "I outgrew him."

So where do you go from here? You redefine what you are looking for. A knowledge of yourself is the best place to start. What do you really want and need from a man? What kind of relationship will contribute to your happiness? What kind of activities and lifestyle are really important to you?

Most women can easily define what they don't want. It's much harder, but also much more important, to define what you do want.

I am reminded of a cartoon which I clipped from an issue of *New Woman* magazine. The cartoon, drawn and conceived by J. Kohl, depicts a woman reading a bedtime story to a little girl. The little girl asks, "Why did Snow White marry the prince? It appears to me that any one of the seven dwarfs was substantially more interesting than a handsome yet boring prince."

For today's woman, that translates to the following. If what you really think you want and need in a man is a college-educated professional, why are you dating auto mechanics? And if what you want and need is a good companion with whom you can share the activities you like, why are you dating someone who hates to do the things you like to do? And, if you are in one of the above situations or something similar, why are you continually arguing with him about it? You don't have the right to change another person, or to even ask him to be different than he is. Let him be and he will be happier and so will you. Seek someone who already has the qualities you find necessary in a man. When you find him, give it your best shot.

You have no right to expect anyone to meet your needs, but you do have the right to have your needs met. This is not doublespeak. It comes back to the basic premise of this entire book. The way you live your life is a choice. If you are choosing the "handsome yet boring prince," you are engaging in the same kind of trophyism that you complain about men doing. Then you complain that he doesn't meet your needs. You traded-off. You gave up stimulating for handsome. Some women give up emotional warmth and comfort for dollars. Some give up understanding and companionship for power. And some get what they want and need by choosing a man who has what they want and need to give. It's a matter of priorities. So be kind to yourself and take a real good look at the person you are and the qualities a man would have to have to fit that person. Both of you will enjoy it more and each of you will probably end up having your needs met.

I would recommend that you read Judith Sill's book, *How to Stop Looking for Someone Perfect and Find Someone to Love*. She suggests exercises which will help you to define what you really need emotionally and psychologically from a relationship if that relationship is going to enhance your life and give you satisfaction in return for the energies you give to it. She notes that we are still choosing mates with a "caveperson" mentality — man as protector and provider, woman as homemaker and procreator. Since women can provide for themselves, this is no longer appropriate. We no longer need protection from wild beasts and men are fully capable of clothing and feeding themselves. The survival of the species is not in jeopardy so procreation can be either a one-person or two-person choice (remember artificial insemination and adoption).

Once you begin to base your choices on the emotional and psychological satisfactions you want from a relationship, not only do you have a better chance for relationship success, but you increase your number of male options. Judith Sill makes a suggestion which goes something like this. There are ten single men available to you. Two are the ones everyone wants, two are not wanted by anyone and the six in the middle are ignored due to some perceived image problem. Her suggestion is that we begin to focus on the men in the middle, those almost desirable ones who are under six feet tall, a little paunchy, slightly bald or whatever. By making an effort to meet these six, you increase your odds of connecting from twenty percent to eighty percent (of course, you will still try for the two most desirable).

This does not mean that you should settle for less than what you want or need. It means that you begin to look beyond pretty packaging and concern yourself with what's inside.

I can feel and hear your negativity in response to the above. "Men don't do that, so why should we?" Have you lost sight of your purpose? I thought you wanted to meet people, especially people of the opposite sex, who will enhance and enrich you life. And, if marriage is your goal, wouldn't you rather have a person you can relate to instead of one who is only pleasant to look at or one who makes other women envy you. I thought you wanted to make choices that would create a satisfying and enjoyable life for yourself. Complaining about the unfairness of the attractiveness double standard won't accomplish that. Choosing for it will.

If you have dated a lot or have been married before, you probably already have some idea of what you need in a man to make a satisfying and enjoyable relationship. Write those pieces of information down. In effect, you are going to design your own ideal man. Get real specific. Look first at yourself, then at how a man can fit you. For instance, I love to read and do a great deal of it. Reading inspires my thinking and incites my curiosity. I need a man who is intelligent and enjoys discussing ideas. I am a self-comforter and a nurturer. I don't need someone to make decisions for me. A man who needs to be in charge turns me off. I need one who respects my ability to think for myself and yet can be available to me on those occasions when I do need comfort and attention. I enjoy a wide variety of activities, everything from baseball games to opera. I don't want to stop doing any of them. I need a man with the same versatility.

Once you have designed the ideal man for you, rank the characteristics you have listed in the order of their importance. You must leave room for compromise. You won't get everything you want so go for the most important and find ways to get the others for yourself. As an example, if a man doesn't enjoy the opera but fits in most other ways, I can attend the opera with other friends. The important factor here would be to make certain that he would not object to my doing so. Again, you do not have the right to expect anyone else to meet your needs, but you do have the right to have your needs met.

In order for this to happen, the man you choose must match in a majority of the areas you describe. Otherwise, why would you want or need him? If you are going to do it all yourself anyway, why bother? Nothing is more alone than being alone with someone. Look for someone who more closely matches your ideal. That's what getting involved is all about.

You'll note that nothing in the preceding paragraphs has anything to do with money, power or physical appeal. It has much to do with being a nice guy. By truly defining what you need, you change your ideas of what is acceptable to you. You also increase the size of the pool of people you have to choose from. That is what I was referring to in Chapter 2 when I hilighted *no one acceptable to you*. Your ideas of acceptable may need to be adjusted as you become a more confident chooser for your own happiness and success. When you redefine your ideas of perfect, you increase your choices. You will not find perfection, but you may find what you need for a satisfying, ongoing and loving male-female relationship. As the saying goes, "The secret to a successful relationship is to find someone who has a set of problems you can live with."

One final comment. Sometimes we try to make a man fit the image we are looking for. We say he has "potential." Let me remind you that potential is just that

— potential. It is not reality, and it may never be reality. As Margaret Atwood says in her book, *Cat's Eye*, "Potential has a shelf life." What you see is what you get and making excuses for a man's behaviors toward you isn't the same as having your needs met. "He just doesn't know how to handle these situations," excuses him. And that's okay if you can live with it, but you must know that your comment shows that you are aware of the lack. If you can live without this particular type of support, okay. If you can't, look elsewhere. Just because he has potential as a mate doesn't mean that the reality will be satisfying.

This chapter was called "Attracting Men" and you probably thought that you were going to get information on how to be appealing to the opposite sex. You did. The bottom line is that you must be yourself and go after the kind of man you want. Attracting men is an active process, not a passive one.

Chapter 14
DATING

What's a date? Silly question? Not really. Not if you look beyond the definition and ask about the purposes of dating. Most of us can agree that a date means we have agreed to spend some time doing something or other with a member of the opposite sex. That something could be dinner, a movie, a sporting event, watching TV, going for a walk, whatever. The possibilities are endless. The real issue is not the date but why a person agrees to a date and what it means to each of the persons involved.

Dating has many purposes including the following:

- To have a good time with a member of the opposite sex.
- To get comfortable being with members of the opposite sex. Practice.
- To attend an activity with another person.
- To define what one is looking for in a man or mate.
- To develop a relationship.
- To find a mate.
- To provide opportunities for sexual activity.

Perhaps you can think of more, but these seven

seem to be the major ones. Each of us gives priority of purpose to one or more of the seven according to our stage in life, our goals and the person we are dating. Let's look at each of these factors before we look at dating itself. First, the stage of life a person is in. Dating is considered to be a normal rite of passage in the American society. It is "supposed" to start in adolescence as a way of getting comfortable with the opposite sex so that we can eventually define what we are looking for in a mate. All of the articles, studies, books, lectures and seminars that I have read or attended suggest that a person needs to date a variety of people during adolescence and early adulthood. Dating many people during these years provides an opportunity to evaluate our reactions to men and to ourselves in male-female situations. It can also help us to develop social skills and confidence.

This process works for some and doesn't work for others. Those women who have difficulty getting dates, regardless of the reasons for it, generally end up with low self-esteem based on the less than positive reactions from members of the opposite sex. Unfortunately, this lowering of self-esteem doesn't go away easily. Many women continue to feel badly years after high school graduation because they weren't able to get a date for the prom. In middle-age, many of these women make a point of losing weight and doing a complete make-over before attending a class reunion so they can show the guys what they missed.

For those women who experience early success in the dating game, the results may be marriage at a young age which prevents them from getting further education, locks them into a lifestyle similar to mom's and dad's, and perhaps, is based on pregnancy. There's nothing wrong with any of these results except that they usually don't involve choice, they just happen. A majority of these marriages end in divorce. This scenario has not changed over time. A large percentage of all marriages will end in divorce. For couples who marry before the age of twenty-five, the divorce rate is even greater.

When divorce occurs, we return to the stage of learning about the opposite sex and ourselves in relation to it. We redefine ourselves and our objectives in relationships.

Another factor which must be considered when discussing the process of dating is our goals. If dating is seen primarily as a way to find a spouse, we approach it quite differently than we do if we are just going out to enjoy another person and some pleasant shared activity. If your goal is marriage, you become more or less selective depending on your view of self. If you see yourself as a chooser, you choose to date only men you would consider marrying. If you see yourself as a victim of chance, one who must wait to be chosen, you will date anyone who even comes close to being marriageable.

In either case, you are no longer talking about dating, you are talking about courtship. What's the difference? Courtship is more intense and involves a series of steps which hopefully lead to the altar. Along the way, a committed, loving relationship is supposed to develop.

If, on the other hand, you are dating for fun, practice or any of the other purposes, the approach to dating is more open and you can date a variety of people regardless of whether or not you would consider marrying any of them.

The final factor, the person you are dating, is also a crucial consideration. Women tend to categorize men. A man may be (1) marriage material, (2) a socially acceptable escort for events, (3) fun to be with, (4) good practice in preparation for the right man, (5) a pleasant way to get free or shared cost dinners, plays, concerts and movies, or (6) an acceptable bed partner.

Because dating can have several purposes and is based on our goals, our stage of life and the availability of a variety of men, many women have a great deal of ambivalence about dating. Most of that ambivalence has to do with negative attitudes caused by a lack of success in either getting dates or in making dating relationships work or in achieving the goal of marriage. I have even had women say to me, "What's the use of dating? I never end up with anyone I want to be with." Or, "What's the use of dating? It never turns into anything." Some women even qualify their aversion to dating by saying they hate the first few dates with a man. I guess it's no fun until they are sure it's worth the investment, until they're sure an ongoing relationship will result.

You already know what I'm going to tell you about those statements. Attitude is everything. If the approach to dating is less than positive, the outcome of dating is going to be less than positive. We create our own reality.

Let's look at each of the negative approaches. First, what's the use of dating? That's negative all by itself without adding any qualifiers about the man or the possibility of a relationship. If anything other than pleasure and shared company is a goal for you in the first few dates, you have set yourself up for failure. During this early phase, you have no right to expect anything more than a pleasant period of time with a member of the opposite sex. When dating becomes a relationship, then you can think about the steps involved in the courtship process.

Those people who hate the first few dates are making it very clear that they are only interested in a relationship, not in having a good time. In effect, they build in failure by putting pressure on the man to be something in their lives that he may not be ready to be. One date is not a relationship. It is a chance to get to know another person better so that you can decide at some point whether or not you want to form an ongoing relationship and what the nature of that relationship will be. In the beginning, it's a one person choice for each of you. Each decides if he or she wants to see the other again based on his or her own purposes for dating. If you had a good time, you want to do it again. If not, you don't. Each of you decides this alone. After the two of you have been dating for a period of time and have seen each other in a variety of situations, you can begin to make relationship decisions together. The better and longer we know someone and the more we share with them, the more involved we become. You can't go from one date to the altar, or at least you won't if you have any sense. Making a relationship and finding a mate takes time, lots of it. See the seasons, all four of them, at least once before you make wedding plans. The first date is too soon for that.

Perhaps the disillusionment many women experience in dating is caused by disappointment. Not current disappointment, but past ones. They have been through this before. You know what I'm talking about, the anticipation and excitement a woman feels when she starts to date a new man. Unfortunately many men do not meet her expectations. So the woman is disappointed in her hopes that this date will be the beginning of a relationship. She then decides that she doesn't like going through the preliminary steps, those dates it takes to get to a relationship.

Again, attitude is the answer. If you can remind yourself that you will have to kiss a lot of frogs before you find the prince, you will get an entirely new perspective on the process of dating. If this frog doesn't turn out to be the prince, maybe the next one will.

With this attitude, each new date will become an adventure, a chance to get to know a man better, to have some interesting conversation, to do something you wanted to do. I'm assuming you follow the oldest dating rule in the book. Always do something you want to do on the first date. That way, even if the man disappoints you, the activity won't.

Even if you have an awful time on the date, think of how much fun you will have telling your women friends about the terrible experience you had.

Many women create disappointment in dating because they are looking for "love." If you are looking for love, look to yourself. Love with and for others starts with love for self.

The successful single woman is not looking for love. She already has it. She loves herself and knows that love between a man and a woman develops over time. Love at first sight is a romantic illusion. We can have romantic interest at first sight or sexual response at first sight, but we can't have love at first sight. That whole concept is simply an image reaction — someone we see appears to fit the image we have of the man we want. We can't really know if the reality of the person fits the image until we know the person better.

This is a good time to deal with a definition of love. I know you don't want to define it, you want to feel it. However, love that lasts is more than a feeling. It has many components, one of which just happens to be emotional, but it also involves human characteristics like honesty, respect, commitment, communication, caring, mutuality, sincerity, openness, common interests, intimacy and trust. How can you know if those things are present without taking the time to learn about another person in a variety of situations and environments?

Love is the concern a person has for another's well-being and happiness. It is based upon and is equal only to love for self. You cannot love another person more than you love yourself. The ability to love comes from within you. You will feel it and treat others in a loving way based upon your relationship to you, not your relationship to them. The only difference between the love we have for our parents, our children, our friends and others and the love that we have for a man is that male-female love relationships involve sexual activity. Whether that love is romantic or not depends upon your definition of romance and the efforts you make to create it. Your enjoyment and success in dating will improve significantly if, instead of looking for love, you look for men you can relate to in a positive and satisfying manner. The nice thing about this approach to dating is that you tend to present yourself more positively and actually increase your chances of finding love, or a long-term relationship, or a spouse, or whatever it is you want out of your relationships with men.

If being in love feels good (and we all know that it does), then not being in love feels bad, right? That's one of the problems in looking for love. If you don't find it, you feel bad and begin to develop a non-loving attitude toward yourself. "If I were a desirable woman, some man would want to love me." Since one currently doesn't, you feel bad. That's a stupid waste of energy. It gets you nowhere. You are lovable even if no man is currently in love with you. End of discussion.

Okay, you have your attitudes adjusted, you are attractive and confident, you're ready. Now what? All dressed up and no place to go? Sure there is. You just have to discover which of the avenues you want to take to get there.

Question. Where are all those statistically evident, available men — the ones who aren't weird, married or gay? Answer. Everywhere. They are in all the places women are, waiting to connect just like the women are. Yes, men do want to date and form relationships just like women do. In fact, men are more like us than they are different from us. If you talk with them about dating and relationships, you will find that men feel the same exasperations and concerns that women do. They just don't talk about them as much and they tend to focus on their personal positives more than women do.

You can meet men anywhere if you are open to doing so. However, you must be certain that your openness shows. This can be done with a smile, eye contact, words and a general attitude of friendliness. If a man starts a conversation with you, respond pleasantly. If he doesn't, speak pleasantly to him and get a conversation started. If you are hesitant to do this, maybe you need to use some of the less direct avenues which are available for meeting members of the opposite sex. If you can't initiate contact (you are the chooser, remember) at the library, drugstore, gas station, church, airport, office, wherever, perhaps one of the avenues described in the remainder of this chapter will work for you.

Personals Ads. Sometimes called companion connections or singles scene ads, they are exactly that — advertising. A person writes a description of himself or herself and what he or she is looking for, has it published in a magazine or newspaper and waits for responses. Whether you answer an ad or place one, the guidelines are the same. (1) Be honest. (2) Read between the lines. (3) Believe what people say.

Be honest. Don't say you are 5'6" and weigh 125 pounds if you actually weigh 200 pounds. You can't possibly lose that much weight in the time between the appearance of your ad and the responses you get. I know men lie, but that doesn't give you permission to do so. Men lie about their height, women lie about their weight. Neither works. When we meet the person, we know the truth and also know immediately that the person is less than truthful. If you have a weight problem, just don't put anything about weight in the ad or in your response to a man's ad.

Read between the lines. If someone doesn't describe a type of employment, maybe it's because he's not employed. Usually it means that the employment is in a blue collar occupation. If he writes wealthy, he probably is not. Or he has low self-esteem and thinks that money is his only appeal. Don't pay attention to the word attractive. Who is going to advertise himself as unattractive? Everyone who places an ad is attractive.

Believe what people say. If he says he likes camping and boating, he does. If you don't, this one is not for you. If he says he wants a non-smoker and you smoke, forget it. Why set yourself up for rejection? Use your energy to connect with someone who shares your interests and activities.

Whether you write the ad or respond to one, leave sex out of it. Phrases and words like loves to cuddle, sensual, or sexy give the impression that a physical relationship is the primary objective of the male-female connection.

Responding to an ad is easy. Most ads now require a telephone rather than written response, so dial the number, and follow the recorded instructions. Just give your first name, phone number and a brief description of you and the things you like to do. Remember to speak slowly and clearly when stating your phone number so the person you are responding to will be able to write it down correctly. You don't need to detail your life story. If he's going to answer, a short message will get his interest, particularly if its pleasant and positive in its approach.

When he returns your call, be pleasant. If he turns out to be someone you are not interested in, don't put him off with a "why don't you call me later in the week" statement and then pray that he loses your number. Instead, when he suggests that you get together, tell him pleasantly and politely that he is not the person you are looking for. Find your own way to do this, but do it. Anything else is unfair and lacks integrity. If you don't do it up front, you'll have to do it later and both of you will end up feeling bad.

If you placed an ad and are responding to calls from men, evaluate the calls carefully. Select the ones you find appealing and start dialing. Again, be honest and base your decision about meeting each man on your gut feelings and your purposes for dating.

If you do agree to a date with someone from the personals, do it in a safe way. When you are determining the time and place to meet, make it one where you will feel safe and comfortable. Each of you should get there on your own. The first meeting should be planned as a brief encounter. You can always extend the time if you want to, but anything more than a meeting for coffee or a drink can be difficult to get through if you end up not liking the person. Give yourself some back-up. Make sure a close friend or relative knows where you are going, who you intend to meet (full name and description) and the time you intend to return home. Plan a specific time when you will call your back-up and prepare a signal that will indicate that you are either safely home or that you are okay where you are with this person. I hope that these precautions will turn out not to be necessary, but as your mother told you, it's better to be safe than sorry. If you feel comfortable with this person and choose to make a second date, you can be more relaxed about arrangements.

I have both placed an ad and responded to ads. I have met some very nice men, a couple of whom have become very good friends.

I have also had some very strange experiences related to these ads. You must be careful. The movies and books that deal with danger through the ads are only fantasy but the message they present is real. Be careful.

Several of my friends have met men through the ads that they have dated for long periods of time. I have heard of people who married others that they met through the personals. So it's worth a try, but give it a real try before you make any judgments about its value for meeting men. You only need to connect with one man to call it successful. That means that you must respond to more than one ad or contact more than one man who responds to you. I believe in numbers; the more you contact, the greater your chances are of connecting. If you respond to two ads and only one man calls you, your choices are limited. If you respond to four and two call, you still have a fifty percent response rate, but the number of men you have spoken with has doubled. So respond to any who are in your acceptable age group, who have the qualities you are looking for and who share your interests and activities.

The Internet. Given the potential for weirdness this option offers, I'm not recommending it. I am aware of only one marriage that resulted from a meeting on the internet. If you think you have found your soul-mate on your computer screen, I would multiply all of the personals ad cautions by about 200 before agreeing to an in-person meeting.

Singles Clubs or Groups. These can be anything from a local community or church group to something nationwide like *Parents Without Partners*. They may be organized around a particular activity like skiing, tennis or travel. I am not a joiner, but I occasionally attend one of these groups if they are dealing with an interest I have. I once joined one because it not only involved a nice group of people in my age group, it also offered something I had been seeking for a long time — a book discussion group.

If any of the groups or clubs in your area suit your needs in ways other than meeting men, they can be useful for social networking. The ones I have looked into seem to be more about social activities than they are about connecting with the opposite sex. However, that is equally important. It gives you an opportunity to develop relationships and to practice social skills as you make new acquaintances, companions and friends of both sexes.

While I have dated men I have met through a singles group, this is not what generally happens. The same people seem to attend the events regularly and after a few months, it's like getting together with old friends. If a new man or woman enters the group, he or she receives a lot of attention for a while, but they eventually settle in and become one of the bunch. Still, it's worth a try.

Special Interest Groups, Classes, Programs. Community theater groups, church activity groups and the like involve both married and single people and can be another way of meeting members of the opposite sex. The same is true of classes and seminars you might attend through a variety of sources such as adult education programs, art museum programs, colleges and universities. I wouldn't suggest that you use these avenues unless you have a genuine interest in the activity, class, seminar or program. You may not meet a man you can date (although you may meet some lovely people of both sexes) and you will have wasted time, energy, and possibly money, doing something you didn't really want to do. However, it could happen. I once met a very interesting man at a lecture series on classical music.

Singles Dances. These activities are usually well attended by members of both sexes. People say they come for the dancing, but most are also hoping to connect with a member of the opposite sex. Yes, there are some who go just because they love to dance, but it always seems to me that there are more people standing and drinking than dancing. In fact, many of the people in attendance refuse to dance when asked. This is true of both men and women. And it confuses both men and women when they ask others to dance and get a refusal. I still haven't been able to figure out why people go to a dance and don't participate. Many of them don't even talk to anyone. They spend the whole evening standing, drinking and not talking. Doesn't sound like much fun to me. Also, doesn't sound like a good way to meet members of the opposite sex. For those people who are willing to meet, dance and talk with others, it can be a way to meet men and I know of several women who have been successful in doing so. However, you will probably enjoy yourself and your evening more if you go with the intent of dancing and socializing and consider it a bonus if you meet someone you end up dating.

You will need to try a number of different dance scenes to find one that fits you. Some of them are no different than the pick-up joints you are trying to avoid. I went to one where I was seriously propositioned twice in the first thirty minutes I was there. I have gone to other dances where I had a wonderful time dancing and socializing with a variety of people.

As with all of the options you have for meeting men, you must be approachable and receptive to meeting others. If you only want to meet certain kinds of men — the tall, good-looking ones — you may not meet anyone and you may not do much dancing either. If no one asks you to dance, you must be willing to take the initiative and ask a man to dance with you.

I suspect the reason people refuse to dance is that they are afraid that they will get stuck with someone they don't want to be with for the rest of the evening. If you don't want to stay with someone, simply thank him for the dance and move on. If that doesn't work, tell him you would like to meet some other people or that you came to mingle. And, if a man dances with you and does the above, please don't feel rejected. It was only a dance, you weren't left at the altar.

Should you go to the dances alone or with another woman? Do whatever feels more comfortable to you, but remember that you will not be as approachable when you are engaged in conversation with a friend. The advantage of going with someone is that you have back-up of the kind that you arranged when dating someone from the personals ads.

Singles Bars. I can't find a lot of positive things to say about this method of meeting men. I tried several singles bars in my area in preparation for writing about them. I talked with both men and women in each of the settings and was not impressed with the information I got. I had heard that these places were pick-up joints and that description was given validity through my experiences. I discovered that there are two types of places — ones where socialization is possible and ones where it is not. In bars with music, conversation is almost impossible because the music is so loud that one must shout to be heard.

Age is a factor in the bar scene as well. If one is under 25, the socialization aspect is different because the majority of people in the bar are likely to be single. Over the age of 25, approximately 50% of the men will be married; over the age of 35, about 75% will be married. Most of them readily admit it. It doesn't seem to make much difference to a lot of the women.

Few of the people I asked admitted that they came to pick up members of the opposite sex. Most said they came to socialize. Some said they came to dance. The majority of people in each of the places with music were doing neither. In the places without music, a lot of talking was going on.

I could have gone home with a man on a number of occasions if I had chosen to do so. I was told by several people that the whole process of picking someone up in a bar is known as "sport f____." Its only intent is a one-night-stand, a score. When I asked people who said they came to socialize and dance if they had ever dated anyone they met in a bar for any length of time, most said no. Several admitted to having picked up members of the opposite sex for sexual liaisons and nothing more.

I did have a pleasant time during my evenings in the bars without music because I enjoyed the social aspects and I met some very open, fun people. The loudness of the music in the other places caused me to limit the amount of time I spent in each. I would not recommend bars as places to meet men for potential dating relationships, but I will leave that choice up to you. If it works for you, do it. However, I believe that the possibilities for success are severely limited. I would encourage you to go with a trusted friend to remove the temptation to leave with a desirable man. He could turn out to be the "area strangler," married or diseased. If he's really that desirable, give him your phone number. If he calls you to make a real date, you may have someone worth pursuing.

Video Dating Service. I belong to a video dating service and I enjoy it tremendously because it truly presents an opportunity for choosing. The only way people meet each other is through mutual choice. When you join, you fill out a profile sheet telling who you are, what you like to do, and what you are looking for, along with other pieces of vital information like age, height, weight, number of children and religion. The profile, along with photos of you, is put into an alphabetically listed book using your first name only. You also make a five to eight minute video in which you are asked about a variety of topics. You choose the topics and questions to be asked by the off-camera interviewer. Once all of these pieces are in place, you can begin to select members of the opposite sex and they can begin to select you. A postcard is sent to each person selected and that person comes into the offices to read the profile and view the video. If the selected person agrees, phone numbers are exchanged and one or the other of you makes a phone contact. If the two of you agree, a meeting is set up and you go on from there.

There are two drawbacks in this situation. One is cost. Video dating services are expensive; not prohibitive, but expensive. The second is that you have to be able to accept a no from someone you have selected without feeling rejected. Everyone you select won't say yes, but you won't say yes to everyone who asks for you either. It seems to balance out. There is one other temporary problem built into this situation. In the beginning, new members are looking for perfection. Since they have paid money, they feel that they have the right to get everything they are looking for in a member of the opposite sex. This is not possible. New members discover this fact within a month or two and settle into a more reasonable evaluation of others.

Why do I like this method of meeting men? First, it's fun. When I go to look through the books, I call it "man shopping" because that's what it is. Second, it's a choice situation. You get to choose the men you want to meet and you get to choose not to meet men who don't appeal to you. Third, it let's you get information about others without a lot of risks. By the time you meet someone, you already have a lot of information about the person and know that you have some things in common. Through video dating, I have met and dated a number of men and have had some very pleasant experiences. I have met some men that I have dated for a period of time. I have also met some men for whom I did not feel a sense of romantic connectedness, but that I liked immensely. They have become friends and are now part of my social network. All in all, if you can afford it, I highly recommend this avenue.

Computer Dating. I have never tried this one and probably never will. Information about you is fed into a computer profile and the computer then selects men it "thinks" you might find compatible with your needs and goals. I don't believe that a computer can factor in the human qualities and nuances of me or of a man who might interest me. If you want to try it, go ahead.

Blind Dates. I'm not sure that blind dates deserve the bad reputation they have developed over the years. My experiences with them have been very positive. In fact, I dated a man I met on a blind date for several years. He is a very positive and pleasant memory for me. We were wonderful social companions and friends for each other. Together we attended a variety of social events and activities and enjoyed each other's company tremendously. He is now married and I am very happy for him. I hope that I shall always know him. I know that I will always think of him fondly and remember him as one of the best friends I have ever had.

The other experiences I have had with blind dates did not lead to long term relationships, but they were nonetheless, very positive experiences. I think the quality of a blind date depends upon the person arranging it. If you know and like the person arranging the date well and trust their judgment, it's probably worth taking a chance. Blind dates have experienced a comeback in the last decade. For young professionals who have little time to spend meeting people in the other ways noted in this chapter, asking friends to introduce them to any single men they know has become an acceptable way to meet members of the opposite sex.

Supermarkets, Book Stores and Laundromats. These options have been added to the old "walking the dog" suggestions listed in magazine articles on where to meet men. Late nights are suggested for meeting men in grocery stores and Sundays for the book stores. If they work for you, fine. Each has built-in conversational ploys in that you can ask questions or make comments based upon what you see in his shopping cart or basket or what books and magazines he looks over. The standard possibilities that he could be married or weird still exist, so exercise caution. I'm not sure that the laundromat is a good option unless it is set up like the Launder Bar in Chicago where the restaurant/bar in the facility encourages people to socialize while they wait for the end of the spin cycle.

The ten avenues for meeting men suggested in this discussion have worked for at least one woman or they wouldn't still be around. Choose the ones that feel comfortable to you and include them in your "everywhere" to meet men. Regardless of the avenues you choose, you have to both look approachable and be willing to approach others. The nice thing about these avenues is that they will start your phone ringing. You must admit, it does feel good to have a man call you. Whether you choose to go out with the man or not, just having a male voice coming at you on the phone will make a difference in how you feel about yourself.

To summarize, let's review the information given at the beginning of this chapter. Dating and mating are not the same thing. If your only purpose in dating is to find a spouse, you must acknowledge that this goal orientation will cause you to miss out on a lot of joyful social experiences with a variety of men.

Dating does have purposes other than finding a spouse. The more aware you are of these purposes, the more free you are to enjoy dating for what it is — a chance to engage in fun activities with members of the opposite sex. You can develop an intimate relationship through dating, with or without marriage in mind. All of us want that satisfying sense of connectedness that is possible with a member of the opposite sex. Through dating, you may also be able to develop a comfortable sexual relationship.

It is important to have your reasons for dating clearly in mind and to acknowledge that dating only to find a mate will cause you to exclude many people from your life. If dating is a means by which you enjoy life more, you can open your mind to a lot of different people in dating situations. Again, it's a matter of choice.

Paradoxically, the less focused you are on finding a spouse, the greater your chances are of finding one because relationships have more of an opportunity to be free-flowing and to develop into whatever they are going to be. If your only purpose is to find a spouse, you may put pressures on a relationship to become something that it can never be. You may also find yourself trying to change other people. If you find someone who seems suitable in many ways, but isn't quite perfect, you may find yourself expecting him to become what you want him to be. If you remember the discussions on expectations in dating, you know that you have no right to expect a person to be anything other than what he is.

Approach dating for what it is. Enjoy it. Dating is fun. Dating is satisfying. Dating allows us to be part of activities we might not otherwise have an opportunity to experience. Dating enhances our self image, makes us feel good about ourselves and helps us learn how to get along with members of the opposite sex. All of these functions of dating are valuable in and of themselves. Finding a mate is merely a bonus.

Chapter 15
DATING ETHICS AND ETIQUETTE

This chapter focuses on dating considerations that fall into the areas of ethics, etiquette and common sense. If you follow the suggestions given regarding behavior in these areas, you will end up feeling good about yourself and you will allow any men who enter your life the freedom to be who and what they are.

You will find, however, that it is easier to be ethical, courteous and sensible if you are involved with men who give you the opportunity to practice such behaviors. If dating is to be a satisfying experience, there are some men who should be left out of your dating life. In some cases, these men should be avoided because they will make you feel bad about you. In other cases, they should be avoided because they are not open to the development of a free-flowing relationship and you will end up feeling used and abused. Let's look at each type.

Professional Singles. These are not professional men who just happen to be single. These are men who have made a profession of being single. They are looking for perfection in a woman.

When you start dating this type of man, he goes out of his way to please you and make you feel special. And you do feel wonderful for a while. The feeling won't last long because he soon becomes critical of little things about you. He then moves on to another woman, leaving you hurt and wondering about your lovability. He says he is looking for a relationship and you think you are forming one, but he has no intention of doing anything more than dating you for a while. He is continually on the look out for a woman who may be more perfect than you. You end up feeling rejected and unworthy.

There can be a positive side to this. Most of these men are charming. While you are dating one of them, you will be treated well and wined and dined in style. It just won't last very long and can be very ego-shattering. However, if you recognize him as a professional single, he may give you some fine opportunities to practice your social skills. Just don't invest too much of yourself in an effort to keep him around.

Relationship Incapable. This type of man will treat you well in the early stages of the relationship. When you begin to show signs of love, he will distance you. He can't handle the emotional closeness, so he pushes you away. Each of these men has his own way of accomplishing the distancing process. Some pick a fight. Some say they will call or come over, then neglect to do so. There is always a "good reason" for these behaviors so any complaint you have about them makes you look like a demanding, dependent woman. If you respond to this man's behaviors by pulling away, he makes a concerted effort to get you back. When the possibility of a loving relationship shows itself again, he pushes you away again.

As soon as you see a pattern of "push me, pull me" starting, get out. Really out. This is not a mating dance. This is a very painful game that will leave you feeling jerked around. It is very ego destructive and robs you of self-esteem. You don't need it.

Angry Men Who Dislike Women. If a man has a lot of animosity toward his ex-wife, ex-girlfriend or mother and expresses it openly, he has a problem. Don't sympathize with him and, above all, don't convince yourself that all he needs is the love of a good woman — you. He needs help, but not from you. All you will get from this man is pain as he transfers his anger from them to you.

Of course, you are not stupid enough to stay with a man who hits you or displays a temper so violent that you think he might. Get away, and stay away, from this kind of man. Save yourself while you still can.

Drinkers and Drug Addicts. No comment is needed about men who are obvious about these addictions. You know better than to get involved with them. The borderline drinkers are the ones you are most likely to find yourself involved with. If a man has to drink every day or gets drunk frequently, he has a problem. You don't need to be a part of it. He may have some very fine qualities, but none of them outweigh the problems that will be caused by his drinking. You can't compete with a bottle, so don't even try.

Sleazes. It's easy to get involved with a sleaze. They are usually quite attractive. They're also smooth and charming. They're just not very sincere. Their approach to women has been perfected to a fine art. It's too bad this approach works because you are only a conquest. Once you respond, you will be dumped by this man as he moves on to practice his art on another unsuspecting victim.

Losers and Neurotics. If a man can't seem to get his life together, if he's still trying to figure out what he's going to be when he grows up, you'd better walk away from him. You can't fix his life and you don't need the hassle this man presents. This is a dependent man who isn't ready to form an adult give-and-take relationship. It doesn't matter how good looking he is or how well he seems to treat you, his life is a mess. And yours will be too if you choose to get involved with him.

Married Men. If you like spending all of your Sundays and holidays alone, getting involved with a married man will make that happen. He has a wife. You get what's left over. The majority of married men do not, I repeat — do not — leave their wives. How can you have a truly intimate relationship with someone who is not available to share the events of daily living with you on a regular basis? Who do you turn to in times of crisis? You certainly can't call him at home. Be wary of any man who will not give you his home phone number. Even if you get what appears to be a home number, make sure you see where he lives by the fifth date.

Formula Relater. These men are only a step above the sleazes. I always have a feeling that they have read a book or two on how to please a woman. Or maybe an ex-wife or ex-girlfriend liked something, so they think you should too. They concentrate on doing things they think will please you, not what will actually please you, but what they think should please you. For instance, you are allergic to roses. You've told him that a dozen times but he still brings you roses. Why? Because it fits the image he has of what is supposed to please a woman.

There's no room for true intimacy with this kind of man because he really doesn't know who you are. If a man pays no attention to the things you tell him about your likes and dislikes, he's operating by the book. He is ignoring the reality of you.

Relationship Rushers. These guys start hinting about permanency after three dates. You may feel flattered, but you don't need this man. He may be prone to hasty judgments in all areas of living, which explains why his life is usually in turmoil. He excuses his mistakes by saying, "it seemed like a good idea at the time." A decision about permanency is too big to make quickly. All the facts aren't in and you have a lot to learn about each other. Don't let anyone rush you.

This man may also be rebounding from a broken love affair and you are being used to stop his pain. Once the pain goes, so will you. You will be the transitional woman, the one who helps him get back on his feet so that he can move on to a new life and a new relationship with someone else. How can you know if a man is rebounding? You can't for certain, but you can reduce the risk by asking him how long it's been since his divorce or last serious relationship. Also, watch for signs of too much intensity early in his relationship with you.

Still in Love. Even though it may be a matter of years since a break-up, some men are still in love with a former woman. You can't compete with the idealized image he has of her. Your relationship with him will be wonderful because he will transfer all the intimacy he imagines he had with her to his relationship with you. That is, until the day he realizes that you are you, not her. Then your relationship with him will be over. You will be left hurt and wondering how this could have happened to you.

If he spends a lot of time talking about his ex-wife or ex-girlfriend and telling you how wonderful their life together was, he's probably still in love with her. This man is not rebounding, nor are you a transitional woman. You are a replacement until the day he realizes he still wants her, not you. Then you're history.

Controllers and Manipulators. These men make decisions about how you should dress, act and live your life. Unfortunately, many women are willing to jump through hoops to keep one of these guys around. They change their hair color, style of dressing and way of living. No man on earth is worth sacrificing yourself for. If you have to stop being you to be with him, dump him. He has a problem. Don't make it yours.

Emotionally Unavailable. This man is just slightly less difficult to deal with than the relationship incapable one. He calls himself the strong silent type. I call him frustrating.

I saw a perfect example of such a man on the national news. The network was showing soldiers saying good-bye to their loved ones before leaving for an overseas assignment. One man was shown standing with a woman who kissed him on the cheek. He had a bored expression on his face and was looking everywhere except at her. She was crying and holding him. There was no response from him until he gave her a brief kiss on the mouth, after which he returned to his disinterested stance. Wonderful farewell, right?

I know you want to defend him by saying, "some men just don't know how to express emotion." Well, maybe they should learn. What's the big deal? A warm hug and kiss wouldn't have killed him and it would have left her feeling loved and cared for.

If you can live without emotional support, sharing and comfort, maybe you can live with a man like this.

I doubt it. Words without actions aren't enough in most human relationships. Humans need physical and emotional contact. Babies can die from lack of love. It's called failure-to-thrive syndrome. Adults don't usually die, but they certainly experience a lot of pain from being in relationships with emotionally selfish people. They definitely do not thrive. As I have said before, there's nothing more alone than being alone with someone.

Each of the types of men described in the preceding section makes a satisfying relationship an impossibility. When you recognize that a man fits into one of the categories, it would be wise to take a look at your dating purposes, your stage of life and your goals. You may be able to have a couple of pleasant dates and a few good laughs with some of them, but you definitely won't be able to form a solid, give-and-take relationship. You can't change these men. Don't try. Use your energies to find someone more open to and capable of a mature and mutual relationship.

I hope that these warnings won't scare you so much that you stop being open to involvements with the opposite sex. I know that having to evaluate such qualities makes it difficult to accept dates with an open mind. Don't worry about it. File the information in the back of your brain and focus on having a good time. Since you are operating from a position of choice, you are in control. Also, since you love yourself, your happiness and well-being won't be dependent on a man. In fact, you know you are in charge of your life when continuing a relationship with a man becomes your choice, when a man's response to you no longer affects the way you feel about yourself. So instead of thinking of outcomes, view dating a new man as an adventure. Instead of fearing endings, take joy from the unfolding of a developing human relationship. Be secure in the knowledge that wherever it ends up, it will contribute to your growth as a human being.

Because all relationships involve human beings, it is important to look at the etiquette and ethics involved in dating. You may not feel that the words ethics and dating belong in the same sentence, yet it is the lack of ethical behaviors that creates most of the problems in relationships between the sexes. Honesty is the characteristic we are talking about. It needs to be present from the beginning. Ethical behaviors are necessary from the first encounter to the last. The following section will address some of the areas where ethics are an issue.

Using Others. We all use people. Hopefully, that usage is mutually beneficial. When it is, we don't call it use, we call it give-and-take. Only when a relationship gets out of balance does it become one person using another. As an example, you have already decided that a man you are dating presents no future as a spouse. He obviously cares for you more than you do for him. He loves you; you enjoy dating him. What's the ethical thing to do? Discuss relationship objectives with him. Make it clear that you are aware of his feelings for you and that you do not reciprocate those feelings. He is entitled to this piece of information. It allows him some choice. You have already made your choice, it's only fair to allow him the same privilege. If he chooses to continue dating you, do not pretend that you are growing into a deeper involvement with him. That would be adding insult to injury.

Or you are dating a man who is willing to take you anywhere you want to go at his expense. Whether you have any thoughts of permanence or not, this is not fair. I don't mean that you have to split expenses. That's a decision the two of you must discuss. But if he buys all the tickets, pays for all the dinners, takes care of transportation and parking, maybe even pays for your sitter, you need to do something to bring the situation into balance. I know the pleasure of your company is worth something. The pleasure of his company is worth something, too. (Let's leave sex out of this. Trading on your body is called prostitution. So unless you are a hooker, it isn't appropriate to this discussion.)

The balance I am talking about does not involve matching him dollar for dollar. I'm suggesting that you occasionally buy tickets and take him to something or that you occasionally prepare a nice dinner for the two of you. I'm suggesting that you take him as your guest to events that you are invited to. These suggestions will create a balance that will prevent him from feeling used.

Exclusivity in relationships. Whether you date one person exclusively or not is your choice. But it's not your choice alone, another person is involved. If he expects you to refrain from dating others, and you are not ready to do so, you must make sure he knows this. This doesn't mean that you talk about the dates you have with others. That would be rude and hurtful. You simply let it be known by natural channels, like having other plans when he asks you out for a specific evening. Or telling him honestly if he asks you about seeing others. This is not a game you are playing. It is a human relationship with lots of potential for pain.

You don't have to limit yourself to one man unless you are ready to do so. Having an ongoing relationship with a man provides the comfort of being able to plan social activities in advance, of knowing that you have a date for Saturday night and for every event or occasion. The ongoingness, the sense of connectedness, creates feelings of joy and security, but it is unfair to let a man think he is the only one, if you are dating others. That's called cheating.

Diseases. We will leave the discussion of sexual behaviors for the chapter on sexuality. However, we do need to look at the ethics now. Regular testing for STD's is a must. If you have a sexually transmitted disease, get it treated. If you have an incurable disease like herpes, please practice safe sex and inform your partner in advance. Nothing more needs to be said. This is the only ethical way to operate.

Female Friends. It's not ethical to make a move on a man who is involved with one of your women friends. If her man makes a move on you, it doesn't matter how wonderful you think he is or how attracted to him you are, it's still not ethical. Tell him so. If the two of you want to start something, he needs to end his relationship with her. Actually, his behavior is not only premature, it's pretty sleazy and doesn't say much for his potential in your life. In any case, you must realize that you will end up losing her as a friend if you do not exercise extreme caution.

What if it's someone who used to, but no longer is, dating a friend of yours? I would recommend talking to her. She may not care if you date him, but I guarantee that she will care if you do it and don't tell her.

This whole scenario involves choices and your system of values. Dating a friend's former man will require a close evaluation of the costs and benefits. You need to exercise good judgment and be open and honest if you wish to maintain your female friendship.

That about covers ethics. Now it's time to look at etiquette and common sense. Review the guidelines for dating in Chapter 9 and add the following to them.

When you give your phone number to a man, it is an invitation to call. That doesn't mean that he will call, even if he asked you for the number. If he does, you are obligated to be pleasant. You do not have to accept a date with him. You may be interested, but legitimately busy. If so, when he asks you out, indicate that you already have plans and suggest an alternate day. If you truly are no longer interested and would prefer that he never call you again, find a positive way to tell him so. There is no need to be rude or insulting. Simply say that you enjoyed meeting him, but on second thought, you are not ready to start dating someone new right now or something to that effect which will let him know that you are definitely not interested. Be prepared for this situation. Find your own way to do it, but do it.

The same is true for a man you have dated once or twice but would prefer not to see again. You don't have to tell him what you find "wrong" with him. In fact, that would be cruel and unnecessary. Just tell him that you are not interested in pursuing a relationship with him or that you are involved with someone else or that you aren't past a former lover or whatever you feel would make it clear to him that future calls would not be welcome.

I know you will be tempted to tell him what's wrong with him and why you don't want him, but that's not your right. He has a right to be who and what he is and you have no right to judge anything other than his suitability for a relationship with you. Since you have decided that he is not suited for a relationship with you, leave his ego alone. I know you think you will be helping him, but you won't. He will probably become defensive and say something equally unkind and both of you will feel bad. Leave it alone. If you think a minor change would make him more suitable for you, and you are willing to invest the time and energy, do it in the context of a discussion while on a date. Let him know in a pleasant way that you find a certain behavior irritating and give him the opportunity to change. If he doesn't, make your decision about whether or not to continue the relationship, but leave his ego intact. You would want the same courtesy if the situation were reversed.

What do you do if someone you are interested in or are already dating says he will call and doesn't? Call him and listen carefully to what he says. If he shows little or no interest, there is no reason for you to pursue it further. Go on to someone who has more interest in dating you. If he shows interest, proceed with confidence.

When you ask a man out, do it with class and style. Be definite about what you want to do and when. If he says no, don't get into begging or childish, pouting behaviors of any kind and don't complain about his lack of availability. If this is a man you have dated before, you might ask him if there is a problem and listen openly if he tells you there is. Pay attention to his response. He may have lost interest. In that case, move on to someone else. If he has a legitimate gripe and you are interested in working it through, do so.

I would recommend that early phone contacts be brief. Obviously there is an interest in getting to know one another better or the call wouldn't be taking place. Once you have established a relationship, talk on the phone as long as you want to or can easily give time to. But early on, keep it short. Why? Because your voice and words are the only basis on which you can make an impression. The person on the other end of the line can't see the interest in your eyes, can't see your smile or frown, can't feel the warmth of your touch. Each of you gets sensory input from only one source — hearing. However, correctly or incorrectly, an impression is formed. When a date is made, expectations are already in place and may interfere with your success in this dating situation. (Remember the discussion on first and second impressions from Chapter 9.)

I would also recommend that the first actual date be fairly short. An evening date of two to four hours is enough for the two of you to continue the development of interest in each other. That's all you are doing at this time — looking into the possibilities of a relationship. Make the first date one where you can talk. Movies do not lend themselves to talking unless you go somewhere before or after the film. I would not schedule an all-afternoon date to something like an art fair with a new man. If the second impression of him doesn't match the first, you're stuck for the duration of the date. Those more lengthy dates can come later when you have developed a relationship with each other.

Whether you are on the telephone or on the first date, send clear signals of interest. It is appropriate to say, "I'd like to get together with you" or "I'd like to see you again." Some women will not make such statements because they fear rejection, but it may be hard for a man to know that you really are interested in further contact unless you say so. If you are not interested, you must also make that clear. At the end of a date may not be the appropriate time, but if he asks, be honest about your lack of interest. Just don't send mixed messages. When you encourage a call you don't want, it's no different than a man saying, "I'll call." The expectation is that there is a continuing interest.

If you have been dating someone for a while and find that you are dissatisfied with the type of activities you engage in, suggest some others. I hear many women complain about the habits that occur in dating such as "all we do is go to the movies or out to dinner." If you want to do something different, tell him so. Better yet, buy some tickets and take him. If that doesn't expand your range of activities, maybe you had better take another look at the man. Perhaps the two of you aren't as compatible as you would like to believe.

When a relationship is over, make a clean break. Don't use statements like "I don't want to see you for a while" or "I need some space." Those are merely euphemisms for "get out of my life" and they hurt as badly as the clear-cut ending. In fact, they may hurt more because the person is left hoping that the relationship will go on. Also, if you end a relationship, make sure you really mean to end it. Don't use it as a ploy to get him to realize how much he cares for you.

Ultimatums are equally out-of-bounds unless you are prepared to follow through. Both of these strategies are manipulative and unfair. They also do not bode well for a satisfying, ongoing relationship.

Other unfair statements are any that begin with "if you loved me" or "you know what's wrong with you." If you are having a problem with another person's way of behaving, use I statements, not accusations. An example would be, "I feel hurt when . . ."

What we are talking about here is openness. None of us, male or female, reads minds. We operate with the information we receive and behave according to our interpretations of that information. Unfortunately, communication between the sexes is often unclear and easily misinterpreted. The only way to deal with the resulting misunderstandings is to talk about them without defensiveness or anger. If something bothers you, say so and expect him to do the same. If he doesn't speak freely, but you sense something is wrong, ask him if there is a problem. If you are truly trying to form a relationship with someone, open and honest communication is essential.

In this discussion, we have been dealing with courtesy which can be defined as the concern you have for another person's feelings. In the end, showing concern for the feeling of others is the best way to avoid having you own feelings hurt.

Now, for common sense. It's okay to date someone you wouldn't marry, but it doesn't make sense to stop meeting and dating others. It also doesn't make sense to hang on to someone you have little interest in or to a relationship that brings you little or no enjoyment just because there's no one else available to you right now. There is a danger that inertia will set in and keep you involved in a relationship that is not productive in your life. Besides that, no date periods can be useful for personal growth. They give you a chance to get to know yourself better and to assess the kind of person and relationship you really want. If you panic at this thought, you need to learn how to entertain yourself. You also need to become more secure as a person.

Whether you are involved in a dating relationship or just beginning a new one, it doesn't make sense to abandon your women friends. No man in the world can satisfy all of your needs, nor should he be expected to. Yes, you do have to devote a good deal of time and energy to forming a relationship with a man, but your life is out of balance if there is no room for your women friends.

Instead of dropping your old friends, include your new man in group activities. If he doesn't fit in or objects to this, perhaps you need to take a closer look at him. Your friends are a reflection of you and his lack of acceptance of them or their lack of acceptance of him may indicate significant differences between the two of you.

On the other hand, don't force your friends to accept your new man. If you plan an activity with a woman friend, don't show up with your man in tow. No one wants to be the third party on your date.

Sometimes relations between you and your women friends will be strained by jealousy. The best way to handle this is to show some sensitivity for your friends' feelings. They don't really want to hear about every cute little thing that goes on between you and your new man. Yes, it's exciting and you want to share your excitement and happiness, but you must temper it with common courtesy.

Don't abandon your lifestyle for a man unless you like the one he presents better. In fact, the best of all possible scenarios would be for the two of you to create one together, but that won't happen in the beginning stages of a relationship. In the meantime, you need to maintain your interests and goals and continue to pursue your dreams. Anything else would be unfair to you.

A final note to the discussion on dating — humans are animals and we have a mating dance just as other animals do. Our mating dance also involves approach and withdrawal behaviors, but these behaviors take place over a longer period of time. The dance starts with infatuation, that intense interest in and excitement about a new relationship. It moves into disillusionment where each of you realizes that the other is only a human being after all. If your relationship survives this stage, you have set the scene for deeper involvement which can move into intimacy and then to commitment. It makes sense to allow a relationship to traverse all of the steps of the mating dance before trying to create a lifetime commitment.

Chapter 16
Sexuality

Please note that this chapter is called "Sexuality," not "Sexual Activity" or "Getting Good Sex," even though it will address those topics. The concept of sexuality involves the sex act, but the act is only a small part of one's sexuality. It is an important part of it, but still only a small part. It is only one way of expressing your sexuality.

Sexuality is the way you see yourself as a woman and how you feel about it. You are a woman twenty-four hours a day, every day. How much of your day could you realistically spend having sex? How many days in a row would you actually be interested in doing that? And how would you feel about yourself as a result?

There are many ways to express your sexuality. Choices have to be made by each woman. When I was teaching pre-teens and adolescents, I could usually tell when a girl had her first menstrual period. She would come to school in more traditional female clothing. Instead of her usual denim pants and t-shirt, she wore a dress or skirt and blouse. Make-up and earrings completed her look of the day. After a few days, the jeans came back for some but not for others. I could almost see the decisions being made. For many, sports and other interests won out. For others, the more traditional roles won. For some, the decision was made to include all facets of femininity — the frilly as well as the rugged. Each tried on a variety of roles as she decided the kind of woman she wanted to be.

Today's woman does get to choose the kind of woman she wants to be. The choices are unlimited — ultra-feminine, athletic, outdoorsy, professional or any combination that she chooses. Because of the feminist movement, we no longer have a clear and well-defined image of woman. I'm not sure that we ever did. We had many years in which society imposed an image on us by virtue of the fact that each of us was born with a vagina instead of a penis. Society said that women were supposed to be homemakers, not earners. Women who were not married or whose husbands were unable to support the family were allowed to work outside the home in certain proscribed types of employment. It was okay to be a teacher, nurse, secretary or waitress. It was not okay to be a construction worker, doctor or lawyer. There have always been women who didn't accept society's view, but such women were seen as oddities. They were not considered to be acceptable role models for other women until recent years.

Women were supposed to get fulfillment from being wives and mothers. No, fulfillment is not the right word. Women's fulfillment was not an issue. It didn't matter to society whether she was fulfilled or not. She was supposed to keep a house and raise children. She was supposed to keep her husband happy so that he could and would provide financial support for her and her children. He was the decision maker; she was the supportive nurturer who was going to be taken care of by him. Dr. Dan Kiley expressed it most succinctly in his book, *Living Together, Feeling Alone.* "Women were to be pretty, be patient, be home, and be quiet."

To some degree, the above description has changed. Women now choose the roles they wish to play. Yes, women are still expected to do the majority of homemaking and child care, but we are working toward change in those areas.

We are all aware of the problems that accommodating change has caused. The divorce rate has increased. There are higher levels of stress for both men and women. Our nation is experiencing a child care crisis. In fact, we could fill a whole chapter with the problems. However, all change requires upheaval and adjustment and that process is going to continue for some time. I hope that we are moving to a better place in human history as we make these changes and adjustments.

The bottom line is that we no longer have to accept the traditional definition of feminine that states that a woman is supposed to be a sweet, soft-spoken, subservient peacemaker. She can be an outspoken, assertive choice-maker for herself. Choice is the key word here. Her sexuality can be expressed in many ways and she gets to choose which of the ways fit her. All of them are feminine because a woman is expressing them. The only influences she must pay attention to are the ones that are reflective of her interests and goals, not the wishes of a man.

I once saw a greeting card which depicts the foolishness of self-expression based on an effort to please a man. The text reads:

> "First, he said he liked independent women, so, I played it cool . . . Then, he said he liked romantic women, so, I played it hot . . . Then, he said he liked passive women, so, I played it weak . . . Then, he said he liked strong women, so, I crushed his head."

We don't need to crush a man's head, but we do need to be true to ourselves as we make choices about how we will express out femaleness.

That's what sexuality is — how you express yourself as a female and how you feel about it. You will definitely feel better about being a woman if you are the woman you want to be, not the one someone else expects you to be. I would recommend that you give yourself permission to express your femininity in whatever way feels good to you. That will allow you to come across as a secure woman who likes herself. That will always be attractive. If you are who you are and like yourself, men will find you appealing regardless of the choices for expression you have made.

Your view of yourself as a woman has developed as part of an ongoing process. You are not done yet. You will continue to grow and change throughout life. The process began at the moment of conception when it was determined that you would be a female. Many of today's adult women were born before it was possible to determine the sex of a child prior to birth. Parents operated on hopes of one gender or the other and made plans and developed expectations based upon their desires. If you had the misfortune of being born to parents who valued male children more than female children, you may have a less than positive image of yourself. If your parents valued you as a girl, but bought into traditional roles, your goals and interests may not have been encouraged. You may not have been given positive reinforcement for the expressions of yourself that felt good to you. Instead, you may have been molded into a female who played a more traditional role. If that's the case, reevaluate. Those messages from the past do not have to control your destiny. You can make new choices.

One of the more significant sexuality messages you received had to do with your body and, in particular, your genitals and breasts. How you feel about your body is determined by the guidelines you received from your parents. Children discover their genitals very early in development as part of body exploration. They also discover that touching the genitals brings pleasure. Unfortunately, many parents discouraged such touching and many women grew up thinking of their genitals in a negative way and viewing sex and related activities as "dirty." Some women are still operating on those negative messages and do not give themselves permission to make choices relative to sexual activity that will bring them pleasure.

Another set of messages was planted during puberty. The type of sex education you received had an impact on your expression of yourself as a woman. Many of today's women were taught only about menstruation and were given no information about males and their sexuality. They did receive warnings about men because "men only want one thing." They were told not to have sex before marriage. This incomplete education and the negative messages about men and their intentions have caused many problems in the relationships between men and women.

If you did not receive complete sex education, with information on both males and females, I would recommend that you visit a library or book store and correct this error. I would also recommend that you start talking to men, asking questions, and listening carefully to the answers you get.

There is one other way in which your parents influenced the development of your sexuality. They sent messages with their behaviors. Did your mother enjoy being a woman? What kind of woman was she and how did your father respond to her? Did you see your parents touching, talking, getting physical with each other? If your parents were uncomfortable with the roles they played and with physical displays, you have probably had difficulty selecting a role for yourself and are possibly allowing the expectations of men to affect the way you conduct yourself.

What was the relationship between you and your mother like? Between you and your father? If you were told what kind of woman you should be and received approval or disapproval according to how well you played your role, you may still be giving the reactions of others more validity than your own opinions.

This is the kind of baggage that interferes with free and open expression of yourself as a woman. It's what takes away a woman's power of choice. How can you be in charge of your own life if you are still bound by negative messages from the past?

It's time to take a very close look at your upbringing and to determine which of the messages you received are productive in your life and which are interfering with your ability to be the woman you want to be. Then make choices which will allow you to be more comfortable with the person you are.

Perhaps you were fortunate enough to be reared in a home where you were allowed to express your individuality and to become a person you are comfortable with. If, additionally, you were given complete sex education without negativity and your questions were answered openly and honestly, you probably have a healthy, positive attitude about yourself and feel good about the choices you make for the expressions of your sexuality.

You express your sexuality through your dress, your speech, your demeanor, your employment choices, your relationship choices and your sexual activity choices. The rest of this chapter will deal only with your sexual activity choices. Remember that they are your choices. Regardless of what I may say or others may tell you, in the end, you make all the decisions about the use of your body in a sexual way.

To begin with, there are four sexual secrets we all should share. I call them secrets because single people are hesitant to admit that any of the statements apply to them because, if one is attractive, one "should" be sexually active. Right? Wrong. Definitely wrong.

Secret Number One — You won't die if you don't have sex. It's okay to choose not to have sex even when you are dating someone regularly and frequently. That's what sexual liberation is all about. Along with the freedom to say yes, you also have the freedom to say no.

Secret Number Two — You are still attractive even if you have no opposite sex relationship at this time. This is true for both males and females.

Secret Number Three — Sexless periods are useful. The best time to review the choices you have made and to evaluate the options in your future may be when you are not sexually involved. This may also be a good time to get a complete medical check-up, including tests for sexually transmitted diseases. This period allows you time to review the role sex plays in your relationships and to look at the other ways in which you express your sexuality.

Secret Number Four — All relationships wax and wane. No matter how sexually appealing you and your sex partner find each other, there will be times when your interest in sexual activity is non-existent. This can be caused by a number of factors like illness, fatigue or stress. If a lack of interest becomes chronic, then it's time to look at relationship factors like unspoken anger and resentment. Otherwise, occasional periods of inactivity are normal and do not indicate a lack of love or that a relationship is over.

With this information clearly in mind, let's look at other factors that must be considered when discussing sexual activity.

Attitude. How do you view sexual activity? Do you respond to the question, "is sex dirty?" with "it is if you're doing it right." Is sex dirty? Is it a natural expression of love? Of lust? Is it a form of control over others? Is it a reward that can be used to manipulate men? Can sex be casual? Is it only appropriate when two people love each other? Your answers to questions like these will tell you how you approach sexual activity. The answers can also give you some guidelines for future choices.

Purpose. Why do people have sex? Sexual activity is not unique to humans. In fact, humans do it just like animals — pigs, cows, cats, dogs, whales. All mammals procreate through ejaculation of the male penis in the female vagina. So what makes human sexual activity different? We can do it at any time. There is no mating season for us; we can have sex for reasons other than procreation.

So why do you have sex? To make babies? Because it's fun? Because it releases tension? Because it is a way to express loving feelings and build intimacy? If you answer yes to any or all of these questions, your purposes can be said to be positive.

Sexual activity can also be used negatively. Do you see it as a way to keep a man in your life? Is it a way to manipulate men? To gain control through withholding activity? To reward "good" behavior? Do you use it to build your ego, to "score?" Do you use it as barter, a payback for dinner, the theater or whatever?

If you have your attitudes and purposes of sex clearly defined, it will be easier for you to make choices when faced with the reality of decisions about sexual activity in male-female relationships. Those realities include the answers to the following questions.

Do you have to have sex in a male-female relationship? That's entirely up to you. No one has the right to make this decision for you.

When should you have sex? When you are ready, when you feel comfortable, and when YOU want to. Again, no one has a right to decide this for you. The only guideline I will give you is to have human relationships before sexual relationships. Why? Because when sex enters into a relationship, it takes on a life of its own. People get possessive and begin to develop expectations of each other. If a human relationship is in place, you can at least voice these expectations and perhaps find a way to accommodate them and each other within the relationship. It also allows you the openness to discuss the possibilities of disease and to discuss the methods you will use to prevent diseases and unwanted pregnancies.

Are you committed to a man because you have had sex with him? That's up to you, but you should discuss this with him. Mutual use should be mutual. If this man is just a friend that you have sex with, he has a right to know that. Wouldn't you want the same courtesy and respect?

Do you have to be monogamous? That's also up to you. It will probably be expected of you. And it's wise to be selective because of the possibility of disease, but choices about sexual activity are yours to make.

The answers to all of these questions involve matters of integrity. It comes down to levels of respect and honesty in human relationships, to treating others in the way you would like to be treated. That includes decisions about how much of your sexual activity you discuss with your female friends. Is it fair to discuss intimate details with others? Most men would rather you didn't unless you are telling others how great they are in bed. Beyond that, most would rather you kept your mouth shut.

Now that the topic has come up, perhaps we should discuss what is meant by the phrase "good in bed." There's a lot of talk about what's good and what's not. Most women's magazines do regular articles on the quality of sexual activity. Regardless of what the articles say, good in bed depends on who's in bed with who. Each of us has our own standard, but good in bed can only be defined in one way. I will say a man is good in bed if he does what I want to do, when I want to do it, for as long as I want to do it. Every woman could make the same statement. So could every man.

Good in bed is very individual and it takes time for a man and a woman to create sexual activity that is satisfying to both. Don't expect miracles the first time you have sex with a man. Just as it takes time to get to know another person as a person, it takes time to get familiar with and comfortable with another person's body. When you begin to have sex with a new man, you may experience some sexual ineptitude. You need to learn each other's body and preferences. A level of freedom, openness and trust is required to develop a sexual relationship which is satisfying to both of you. That's another reason for having human relationships before sexual relationships.

What about orgasms? According to most authors and researchers on this subject, the sense of warmth and intimacy that comes from touching and cuddling is just as important. The best of all possible sex would give you both orgasms and intimacy.

If you want really good physical orgasms, masturbate. This is not an abnormal behavior. Masturbation is considered to be a normal, healthy alternative to sexual activity with a member of the opposite sex. Plus that, you know exactly where to touch, for how long and with what amount of pressure to give yourself pleasure.

It's okay for a woman to initiate sex. It's also okay to enjoy fondling and touching without genital activity. The only caution I would give is don't say no when you mean yes. If you really don't want to have sexual intercourse, say so and mean it. If you mean no, you know when to stop the touching and fondling. No one accidentally has sex. It is a purposeful act. I have never seen anyone's clothes accidentally come off, have you? Don't kid yourself. Adults take responsibility for their actions. If you want to have sex, do so and enjoy it. If you don't, say so and act accordingly.

Most people claim sex is better with someone you love, but supposedly, illicit sex is more exciting. Which is right? I suspect both are. I also suspect that a person gets out of sex what he or she brings to it. Good sex requires losing oneself in the act. If it's duty sex, it's probably not going to be very exciting. If it's accommodation sex, it's probably not going to be very satisfying. If it's mutually desired and both persons are actively involved, it's probably going to be pleasurable sex, with each person feeling good about it.

All of the sex experts suggest talking about your sexual needs and expectations in a non-threatening way. Many also recommend sensate focusing to learn about each other's body and the range of reactions each has to a variety of activities. This makes sense since sex is usually a two-person activity. Good sexual relationships are not magic. They are not accidents nor are they created through luck. They happen because two people take the time to know each other well.

Sexual intercourse is only one of the many ways we have of expressing intimacy within a relationship. We also express intimacy through shared friends and social activities, through successful problem solving, and through conversations and discussions about deep feelings and thoughts, along with regular sharing of the details of daily living. Without these kinds of intimacy, you are having a sexual relationship only, not an involved human relationship that includes sexual intimacy.

If all you want is a purely sexual relationship, that's your choice to make. I'm not sure that's possible, but if it suits your needs and you feel good about yourself, that's okay. There is a danger of one or the other of you wanting more at some point. There is also the danger of getting locked into a situation from which it will be difficult to separate yourself without a significant amount of pain and disappointment.

The final note in this chapter is about sexually transmitted diseases. AIDS seems to have claimed the spotlight in this arena, but we still have to concern ourselves with syphilis, gonorrhea, clamydia, herpes, genital warts, pubic lice, trichomoniasis and others. If you engage in sexual activity, you are at risk. If you have sex with a number of different men over time, you increase your risk. The guideline I gave in sex education classes is this — if you have only one partner, get checked or tested once a year. (You don't know what he's doing when he's not with you.) If you have more than one partner, get checked or tested every six months.

Of course, you are practicing safe sex and using a latex condom. (The only really safe sex is masturbation and, even then, you should wash your hands before touching your genitals.) Additionally, you should use a spermicidal preparation with non-oxynol 9, urinate after sex, and wash your genitals after sex. All of these will help to reduce your risk of disease.

Let's talk condoms for a bit. If you are dating, sex is always a possibility. I would suggest that you keep a condom in your purse. Since condoms are individually wrapped, they fit easily into small spaces. Drop a couple into a coin purse or into the zipper pocket of a purse.

Carrying a condom does not mean that you are planning to have sex. It only means that you are acknowledging the possibility and being prepared for it. You lose nothing if you don't have sex. You could lose a lot if you do and have no way to protect yourself.

Choosing not to have sex is one of your options just as choosing to have sex is an option. As you make your choice, keep in mind the fact that there is only one good reason to have sex. *Because you want to*. Not because someone else expects you to, but because you want to. If you remain true to yourself, your choices will always be clear.

Chapter 17
HANDLING HEARTBREAK

A relationship that you have been involved in has come to an end. The possibility that a relationship will not last is one of the built-in risks of involvement. It hurts, but it's not the end of the world. You will not die. No one dies from heartbreak. You will get over this even though you feel like you are going to hurt forever.

There are some healthy ways to handle heartbreak, ways that will allow you to come away from the break-up with your ego intact and your psyche open to another relationship. Let's look at what you are going through and at some of the possible suggestions for handling it.

The most common reaction to a break-up is intense pain. It may be disguised as bravado or anger, but the underlying feeling is one of hurt. Pain and a feeling of emptiness are part of every break-up, even the necessary ones. Yes, some break-ups are necessary because people are hurting and destroying each other through frequent attacks on each other's self-esteem. These destructive relationship break-ups are actually very healthy. That doesn't make them hurt any less, but they can get you to a better, emotionally healthier place if you allow them to.

The hardest ones to accept are the ones in which you thought you had a viable relationship with only a few problems that you were sure the two of you could work out. Obviously, the other person did not think so, or was afraid to try. You don't feel ready for a break-up and the pain is intense.

To handle the hurt, *take care of you.* If you had a bad cold, you would treat it and take some time to get better, so why can't you be as kind to yourself when you have a bad heartbreak? Following are some ways to be kind to yourself.

1. **Acknowledge the pain.** You are human and you hurt. Trying to pretend everything is okay when it's not won't help. You don't have to impose your pain on others, but it is all right to tell friends that you hurt. You are already emotionally tapped out and asking yourself to behave as though everything is fine will exhaust you further, so give yourself permission to feel the pain.
2. **Take a day or two off if you need to.** Be careful with this one. If staying home alone will create comfort, stay home. If work will give you a way to escape from the pain for a while, then go to work. It's amazing what a day of pampering yourself or a day of giving in to depression will do for you. Sometimes you have to hit bottom to get back up. Each person handles it in her own way, and if you feel like not showering or brushing your teeth or getting dressed, do it. If you feel like treating yourself to a massage or make-over, do it. Do what will help you.
3. **Forgive yourself.** Don't berate yourself. You are a good person even if this relationship didn't work. It's too easy to say, "if only I had done this" or "if

only I hadn't done that," it would have worked. You are and were the person you are and you have a right to be that person. If you feel that you really did do something that caused the break-up, forgive yourself. You are human after all. It won't help to tell yourself that there's something wrong with you. If you have done this in previous relationships, resolve not to do it again. If you don't understand why you did it or why it caused the break-up, get some professional help and figure it out. Make the pain you are in count for something.

4. **Forgive him, don't berate him.** I know it seems easier if you can say he's a jerk, but it really doesn't make it hurt less. It hurts because it represents a lifestyle change. If you have been with this man for a while, you will miss him. There is an empty spot in your life. However, if he really is a jerk, why would you want him back?

   Berating him won't make it hurt less and, after all, you chose this jerk. No one forced you to get involved with him. If you have been in a series of such relationships, it's time you talked to a therapist and found out why you keep choosing this kind of man.

5. **Remember that now is not forever.** Forever is too long and too absolute. Just because this relationship didn't work doesn't mean that none will ever work. It is possible for you to find someone else. People do it all the time. You will, however, have to get through this period of adjustment and it won't help to focus on never. Focus on today. This is just one relationship, not your whole life.

6. **Talk to a close friend.** Let someone help you through this. Everyone has been through at least one break-up and can identify with your pain. The support of a good friend who will listen to your hurt and offer comfort can help you through the hours when you are really tempted to call and beg him back into your life.
7. **Give yourself permission to do some weird things.** Like calling him. Like writing him letters. Like sitting in the corner and crying. Remember, I said weird, not vicious. I have read lots of articles on creative revenge and find that most of the suggestions presented only make the avenger look bad. They cause inconvenience and discomfort for the other person, but getting your "pound of flesh" won't stop your hurt. In fact, you will probably end up feeling embarrassed and disliking yourself for the things you do. And it will give him cause for anger which will be focused on you. Is that what you really want?

These seven suggestions will be useful throughout the recovery process, but they won't accomplish the recovery. It's going to take time and you are going to have to do an autopsy.

Everyone does an autopsy when a relationship dies. It's part of getting past the pain. You need to look for causes. You have to put the memories, both good and bad, to rest. And after the autopsy, cremation, not burial, is in order. You will need to distribute the ashes of your memories to their appropriate places.

All of life's experiences contribute to the process of becoming the person you are. If you deny either the pain or the beauty of a relationship, you lose the opportunity it presents for personal growth. That's why an autopsy is necessary. Remember, however, that you can use the autopsy either negatively or positively. The focus you put on it will also determine, to some degree, how it will affect you in future relationships.

So how do you do the autopsy? No problem. Your mind will do it for you. In the first couple of weeks, and perhaps for some time afterwards, you won't be able to stop it. You will continually think about all of the good in the relationship and how much you miss it. You will remember all of the good times and the wonderful things you said to each other, all the precious moments you shared. And the memories will hurt.

Regardless of the hurt, there are rules and proper procedures for doing the autopsy which must be followed completely if you want to come out of this process with your ego intact. If followed to the letter, you may even come out of the autopsy with a very positive sense of yourself because you were smart enough to get this person out of your life before he was able to inflict great emotional harm to you and your self-image.

Rule Number 1 — Face the pain. Denying it will only create fears of getting involved again.

Rule Number 2 — Write some of your thoughts and feelings on paper or put them on tape, not to hurt yourself or to prolong the pain, but to give expression to your feelings about the breakup.

Rule Number 3 — Don't turn this potentially positive process into a negative one. You did have good times. All relationships do, even the worst ones. Saying "he lied or was playing a game" or "it's my fault it didn't work" will make this a negative experience. Blame won't help.

Now for the autopsy itself. It starts with remembering happy times. Little by little, other memories creep in and you begin to recall the bad times or the times when the relationship was less than comfortable. Then you will start to feel angry. This anger is very healthy as it indicates that you are beginning the recovery process. You don't have to vent your anger on the person, but you do have to allow yourself to feel it. After all, this is someone you chose to love and an open expression of hatred will leave you with a feeling of dislike for yourself.

If you are the one who called for the break-up, you may have done it in hurt and anger and think that you dealt with your anger then. You didn't, not all of it. During the autopsy, you have to deal with anger over the fact that the relationship didn't last, that you are now alone, that it has happened to you again. The "agains" are the hardest part because you get angry with yourself and start to blame you. Anger is a necessary part of the unbonding process. Don't turn it on yourself. You want to unbond from your former lover, not from yourself. You don't want to become one of Margaret Atwood's "fallen women." "Fallen women were women who had fallen on men and hurt themselves . . . Fallen women were not pulled down or pushed women, merely fallen."

Relationships are two-people events. So are break-ups, even if you don't feel like you had a choice in the process. It's not anyone's "fault." It just happens for a lot of reasons and you need to investigate the reasons, not assign blame. Sometimes the reasons make sense, sometimes they don't, but you must investigate them to get past the pain. Right now, you are probably saying, "What about women who get beat up or deal with adultery?" Those are reasons, absolutely. But hating yourself or hating the other person will only make you and others around you miserable. So ask yourself the hard questions, answer them honestly, learn from the answers, and then get on with your life.

1. **Is there anything you could have done that would have made a difference?** Probably not. Who knows what turns people off to each other? It usually has nothing to do with the other person. It's usually something within each individual. If it's beatings or adultery, there's still not much you could have done to prevent it. These are choices made by individuals.

    If your answer is yes because you did do something like have an affair or get caught in a serious lie or pick a fight or whatever, examine it, forgive yourself and resolve not to do it again. Go on with you life feeling glad that you have learned something.

    The answer to this question is the hardest part of a break-up. It's what the autopsy is really all about. We are trying to find a way to blame ourselves. Why? Because it gives us some measure of control when everything appears to be out of control. Don't do it. You are still a good person even if you did do something stupid. Even if you discover that you set out to hurt him, you don't need to hate yourself. Seek out a competent therapist and deal with the internal anger which may be causing you to do hurtful things to others.

2. **If this person were available to you right now, would you have him back in your life?** Any immediate answer except yes is not one that would lead you back into a good relationship. It would only prolong the hurt. If it's yes, if he stops drinking or yes, if he does more around the house or yes, if he spends more time with the children, forget it. All require change from him which will only happen if he wants it to.

   If it's yes, and I will work with him to build a more solid way of relating to each other and handling problems, that's quite different.

3. **Why do you want him back?** If your answer is, I don't, take your pain and move on. This is not the right person for you. Yes, it will be painful. No relationship break-up occurs without pain. When answering this question, I would recommend that you ask if your life is better with this person or without him. If it's better with him, do what you have to do to get him back. If it's not, move on.

4. **Do you really have a choice?** It's hard to admit powerlessness, but if the other person dumped you, with or without reason, you are not in control and have to accept that. Your are not, however, totally without power. You have power over you and can use it to rebuild your self-esteem and a more satisfying life for yourself.

5. **Are you holding on to pain?** Are you really trying to get past this or are you wallowing in self-pity? "See this always happens. Why should I even try again?" Sometimes a woman will prolong her pain so she won't have to put her life back together and start over.
6. **Is this man one in a series?** Is this a pattern whereby you choose to be involved with men with whom you cannot establish an ongoing, loving relationship. If so, what do these men have in common and what is causing you to repeat this pattern? If you find you are repeating a pattern of seeking love from unloving sources, seek instead to learn to love yourself so that you can get the kind of man you deserve.
7. **What did you learn from this relationship?** You learned some hard things, some negative things, some painful things, but it will be helpful if you can focus on the positive lessons you learned instead of the negative ones. Let me suggest some lessons you may have learned that would be worth congratulating yourself for.
    - you are capable of loving another person.
    - you were able to engage in a give-and-take relationship.
    - you behaved in a mature and rational manner during most of the relationship.
    - you can recognize factors in a relationship that are predictive of relationship difficulties.

    Yes, you learned some things about the way you behave in relationships and about you as a human being and the qualities you must have in a relationship. The previous examples should get you started on a positive review of the relationship and its impact in your life. Cataloging the positive lessons you have learned will, in an of itself, make the pain of doing the autopsy worthwhile.

8. **Where do you go from here?** That's up to you. You have a lot of options. You can start dating again, you can start a project you've been putting off for a while, you can concentrate on strengthening old friendships or building new ones, you can do whatever feels good to you with anyone you choose. Possibly the worst thing you can do is sit home and brood. Yes, you do need time to mourn and get past the pain, but you do not need to become a vegetable.

   You may not feel ready to date, but socializing with others of both sexes will give you positive feedback and take your mind off the loss. When you feel ready to start dating again, do it. There is no such thing as too soon to start casual dating. There is such a thing as getting involved too soon. That's known as rebounding in which you transfer love feelings from the old relationship to a new man. It may appear to relieve the pain for a while, but you may find yourself in a desperation relationship that leaves you feeling more empty than you did before. Trust that the pain will eventually end whether you enter into a new relationship soon afterwards or not. In fact, if you use the pain to learn about yourself, it can be a very productive period of positive personal growth.

Throughout the autopsy period, be as honest with yourself as you comfortably can. When you finish the autopsy and get back to the business of living your life happily without him, be aware that you will still have an occasional bad day. Over time, your strength will return and you will find that you are once again enjoying life and looking forward to your own future.

Before leaving this topic, there are four truisms that must be noted. They apply to all relationships, not just male-female ones, but a reminder of them is appropriate to a discussion on the break-up of a male-female relationship.

One — the separation of people who have been closely involved is a risk in all relationships.

Two — the degree of pain one experiences following a break-up is directly related to the degree of emotional investment one has in a relationship.

Three — from birth until death, people will move in and out of our lives and our relationships with them will wax and wane during the time of involvement.

Four — sometimes the break-up of a relationship has nothing to do with the other person. Sometimes a person is simply choosing for his or her own growth.

Chapter 18
THERAPY — DO YOU NEED IT?

Do you need therapy? Only you can answer that. Even though I have recommended therapy several times in this book and have been in therapy for several years myself, I don't feel that everyone "needs" it. Therapy is most useful when a person seeks it out for himself or herself. Therapy is an active process that requires openness and honesty and a willingness to look behind the closed doors of the mind. It requires a desire to change as part of an effort to create a more satisfying life for yourself. Therapy takes a lot of emotional effort and a significant commitment of time.

Some people aren't ready for therapy and won't benefit much from the time spent in the sessions. They fight the process by setting up unrealistic goals or by seeking a "quick fix" to complex problems and situations. Or they resist change because of the discomfort that change may bring. Such people aren't likely to benefit significantly from therapy.

When I began therapy, it did not have the acceptance it does now. My close friends told me not to reveal the fact that I was seeing a psychiatrist to others, particularly the people I worked for and with, because it would cause them to have a negative opinion of me. My friends thought that others would question my stability and competence and that they would no longer trust me to handle situations responsibly.

People who seek therapy today are seen in a more positive light. Instead of being viewed as crazy, many are more highly regarded for having the good sense to improve their lives through the process. If concern about the reactions of others is stopping you from choosing some form of counseling, take a closer look. Seeking help from a trained professional is a perfectly acceptable option in today's stress-filled world.

Therapy is expensive, but most insurance companies will pay at least some portion of the cost. A simple call to your insurance company will let you know what benefits are available to you. Some will pay a partial amount with no limit on the number of visits. Some have specific criteria for payment based upon the type of counseling and the qualifications of the therapist you choose. Therapy may be provided by licensed social workers, psychologists or psychiatrists. The type of professional you choose will be based on your goals.

Ask yourself what you expect to get out of therapy. If you are looking for a shoulder to cry on, talk to a minister, priest, rabbi, relative or close friend. If you want to make changes in your approach to living and create more satisfaction in your life, then a more formalized situation my be required.

Your goals in therapy will be related to the reasons you have for entering the process. Your reactions to the questions below will help you to decide if you could benefit from therapy.

1. Are you engaged in repeated self-defeating behaviors? Self-defeating behaviors are any that create new problems or that leave you feeling bad about yourself.

2. Is there a general feeling of unease in your daily existence?
3. Are your relationships with others in a constant state of turmoil?
4. Do you continually berate yourself or compare yourself negatively to others?
5. Do you frequently feel tense or overly emotional?
6. Do you seem to be angry most of the time? Is your approach to daily living filled with hostility?
7. Do you make the same mistakes repeatedly, particularly in male-female relationships?
8. Do you feel out-of-control and unable to set or achieve goals?
9. Are you depressed most of the time?
10. Have you thought about entering therapy many times?

At one time or another, each of us experiences some degree of the behaviors in question, but if you experience any of them for an extended period of time, therapy might be useful.

Therapy is a process. The process involves learning about yourself and accepting responsibility for the quality of your life. It may or may not require you to analyze the effects of past experiences. The therapist guides you through this process. He or she does not control the therapy situation. You do. The therapist guides you in your search for a greater understanding of yourself and assists you in your efforts to change those things in your life which create unhappiness. If the therapist is to fill this role successfully, he or she must be a person you trust and feel comfortable with.

Finding a person who satisfies these conditions is of primary importance if you are going to benefit from your time in therapy. Feel free to say no to therapy with someone who does not meet the criteria for you. There are many other therapists available if the first, second, or even the third, doesn't feel right to you. Choose for you.

I do have to add one caution here. I once had a friend who sampled nearly every therapy available. Individual, group, EST, weekend sensitivity training, you name it, he tried it. He would spend several months with each, all the while proclaiming its virtues. When it appeared change was occurring in his life, he would suddenly stop the one he was in and try another. It seemed to me that he had little interest in personal growth but enjoyed the opportunity to revel in the misery of his life with a new audience every few months. I still run into him about once a year and even though he has made a career change and grown older as the rest of us have, his problems and his reactions to them are no different than they were fifteen years ago.

Therapy is hard work. That's the negative side. The positive side comes from the excitement of knowing yourself better and watching your own growth and development over time. The increasing sense of control you have in your life will make all of the time and money spent an investment that brings returns throughout your life.

If you feel that therapy will be useful to you, do it.

LAST WORDS

Every suggestion offered in this book is just that, a suggestion. The introduction stated that this was to be a book about choices. If you have chosen to make even one change or to do one thing differently, and that effort has brought more happiness into your life, it's been worth the time, energy and expense involved in reading this book. Rather than close with additional promptings to action, I leave you with the following passage to ponder.

> Beyond a wholesome discipline,
> be gentle with yourself.
> You are a child of the universe,
> No less than the trees and the stars;
> you have a right to be here.
> And whether or not it is clear to you,
> no doubt the universe is unfolding as it should.

from *Desiderata* by Max Ehrmann

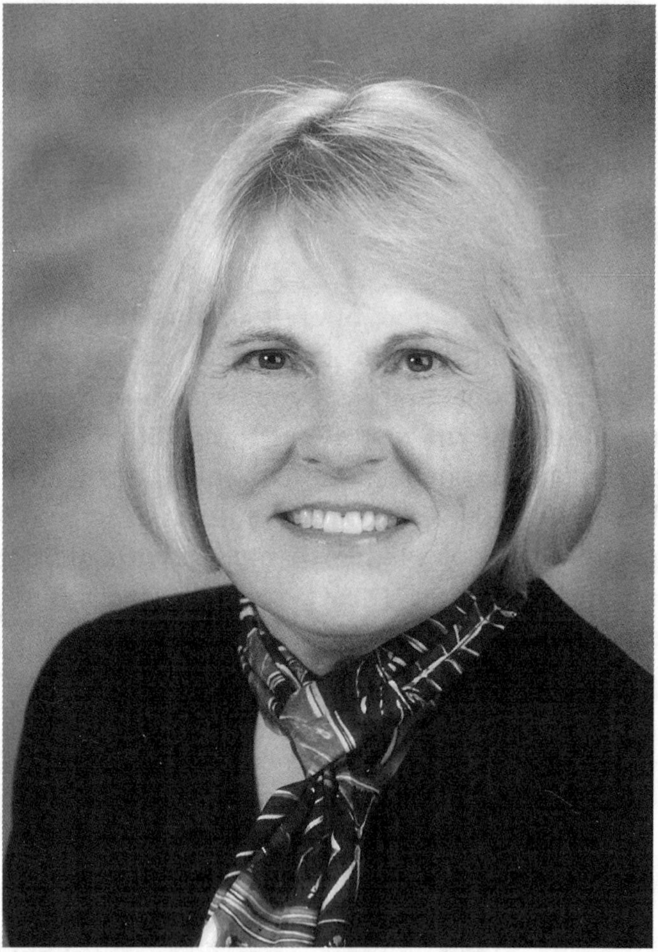

ABOUT THE AUTHOR

Kathy is a single woman living a happy and satisfying life in Chicago. Her career in the field of Human Development has made her an astute observer of people and their relationships to both men and women. The insights she offers in this book will help the single woman to enjoy life whether or not marriage is a goal.

Celebrate your single life!

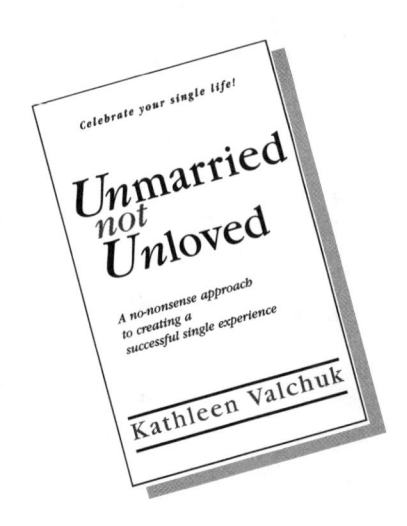

Unmarried not Unloved

A no-nonsense approach to creating a successful single experience

Kathleen Valchuk

Order your copy today!

Name: _____

Address: _____
City: _____
State/Zip: _____

Daytime phone: _____

Send check for $12.95 plus $3.00 shipping and handling to:
(Illinois residents please add $1.13 sales tax)

Lichfield Publishing Company
Suite 406C, 1360 N. Sandburg Terrace
Chicago, Illinois, 60610
312-664-9145   Fax 312-664-9155

Books will be shipped first class mail unless quantity shipment required. Sorry no C.O.D. or credit card orders.

Quantity discounts are available. Please fax or give us a call!

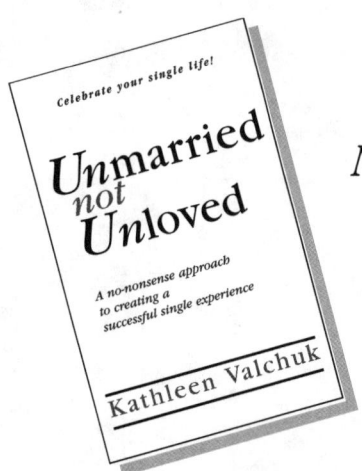

Need an extra copy for a friend?

Name: _____

Address: _____
City: _____
State/Zip: _____

Daytime phone: _____

Send check for $12.95 plus $3.00 shipping and handling to:
(Illinois residents please add $1.13 sales tax)

Lichfield Publishing Company
Suite 406C, 1360 N. Sandburg Terrace
Chicago, Illinois, 60610
312-664-9145 Fax 312-664-9155

Books will be shipped first class mail unless quantity shipment required. Sorry no C.O.D. or credit card orders.

Quantity discounts are available. Please fax or give us a call!